A METHODOLOGY
OF THE HEART

D1601384

ETHNOGRAPHIC ALTERNATIVES

BOOK SERIES

Series Editors: Carolyn Ellis and Arthur P. Bochner
(both at the University of South Florida)

Ethnographic Alternatives emphasizes experimental forms of qualitative writing that blur the boundaries between social sciences and humanities and experiment with novel forms of expressing lived experience, including literary, poetic, autobiographical, multivoiced, conversational, critical, visual, performative, and coconstructed representations. Emphasis should be on expressing concrete lived experience through narrative modes of writing.

Books in the Series:

A METHODOLOGY OF THE HEART

Evoking Academic and Daily Life

Ronald J. Pelias

ALTAMIRA
PRESS

A Division of Rowman and Littlefield Publishers, Inc.

Walnut Creek • Lanham • New York • Oxford

ALTAMIRA PRESS
A Division of Rowman & Littlefield Publishers, Inc.
1630 North Main Street, #367
Walnut Creek, CA 94596
www.altamirapress.com

Rowman & Littlefield Publishers, Inc.
A wholly owned subsidary of the Rowman & Littlefield Publishing Group
4501 Forbes Boulevard, Suite 200
Lanham, MD 20706

PO Box 317
Oxford
OX2 9RU, United Kingdom

British Library Cataloguing in Publication Information Available

Library of Congress Cataloging-in-Publication Data

Pelias, Ronald J.
   A methodology of the heart : evoking academic and daily life / Ronald J. Pelias.
      p. cm. — (Ethnographic alternatives book series ; v. 15)
   Includes bibliographical references and index.
   ISBN 0-7591-0594-4 (hardcover : alk. paper) —
   ISBN 0-7591-0595-2 (pbk. : alk. paper)
   1. College teachers—Conduct of life. 2. Scholars—Conduct of life.
   3. Education, Humanistic. I. Title. II. Series.
   LB1778.P45 2004
   378.1'2—dc22   2003022160

Printed in the United States of America

♾™ The paper used in this publication meets the minimum requirements of
American National Standard for Information Sciences—Permanence of Paper for
Printed Library Materials, ANSI/NISO Z39.48–1992.

For my parents,
Gus and Merle Pelias

Contents

CHAPTER 1

The Heart's Introduction

A *Methodology of the Heart: Evoking Academic and Daily Life* offers a collection of studies on everyday and university life written as methodological alternatives to what one typically finds in academic scholarship. The essays all originate in the desire to write from the heart, to put on display a researcher who, instead of hiding behind the illusion of objectivity, brings himself forward in the belief that an emotionally vulnerable, linguistically evocative, and sensuously poetic voice can place us closer to the subjects we wish to study. In this sense, *A Methodology of the Heart* is a book located in the researcher's body—a body deployed not as a narcissistic display but on behalf of others, a body that invites identification and empathic connection, a body that takes as its charge to be fully human.

To begin a discussion of a methodology of the heart, it only seems appropriate that I would share where my heart is now. I am drawn to this way of working out of a feeling of lack. I feel the lack in those critical arguments tied tighter than a syllogism, those pronouncements given with such assurance, those judgments that name everything but what matters. I know there is more than making a case, more than establishing criteria and authority, more than what is typically offered up. That more has to do with the heart, the body, the spirit.

That lack resides in my body as a wound. As I go about my business of just living and of doing my job in the academy, I never want to hurt or be hurt, but too often I've watched claims of truth try to triumph over compassion, try to crush alternative possibilities, and try to silence minority voices. Seeing the pain this causes, I seek another discourse, one that still has an edge, that could say what needs to be said but would do no harm. I want a scholarship that fosters connections, opens spaces for dialogue, heals. I want to rein in power like one might a runaway horse. I need to write from the heart.

That lack now lives in me as a vow. I promise:

1. to walk, whenever necessary, on broken glass,
2. to rejoice, whenever possible, in the stitch,
3. to carry, whenever needed, the weight of the stone.

This is a way of being in the world. And because I am not the person I would always like to be, I do not always keep this vow. At such times, I disappoint myself and I am ethically suspect.

So I move forward with this preface, a beginning effort that tries to introduce its subject in three parts. In part 1, "The Missing Body," I mark what I think is most often absent from our research. In part 2, "The Playful Body," I identify through a series of heartfelt fragments how the body, that site of feeling, might lay claim to its emotive agency in our research practices. In part 3, "The Ready Body," I point to how I will move forward in the manner I am advocating throughout the book. As I proceed, my strategy is always to put on display a methodology of the heart.

Part 1—The Missing Body: A Sentence Concerning What Is Absent in Scholarly Writing

We could say the heart,

> not the one of Valentine's Day with its lace trimming and perfect symmetrical shape, but the one exposed, raw, deep inside the operating theatre's ribs, irregular, almost vulgar as it pounds and pounds insisting upon its presence—sometimes quietly, sometimes as raucous as crows flying from a grave;

> that slightly off-center heart, filled with its blue blood ready to turn red when it comes to air;

> that symbol of our desire, controlling what gets in and out;

> that swollen orb, ready to burst from its own intensity, worrying and fascinating us all, there, beating in front of us, visible only from the careful and frightening work of those who, like doctors, lay it bare before us, who

place it under the lights for scrutiny, who know how to handle it, to fix it (and it is worth remembering that cutting through its skin may damage before it repairs, that gaining access may startle before it enlightens, that probing what is so central may be just what diminishes it, destroys it);

that voracious fruit that cannot be picked;

or, perhaps instead, we could say the hand,

the opposite one of daily use, the hand that doesn't quite know what it's doing, that struggles to complete the task, that fumbles with whatever it tries to examine;

that curious hand that never believed in *pi* can never get it right, can never hammer the nail on the head;

that soft hand, uncalloused, open as Christ's palm greeting the spike;

that weeping hand, holding the head of a pin for the thousands who might be present to dance on its point, figures its fingers into its own design, pointing, surrounding, beckoning to cast its spell, its myth, its mystery;

or we could say the groin,

that messy place that consumes, but some would say we were just trying to write some kind of titillating sex text instead of realizing that we were trying to find their bodies, trying to bring them back to themselves, trying to be alive; and some would say that that metaphor is just too easy, too familiar, too trite, even though their fascination never stops; and some would say—probably in a deep and breathy voice—that we have finally found the right slot to go about this, found just the right spot, right there, yes, that's the place, there, before we would have to call a halt to whole thing because really we had gone too far, farther than we had ever imagined, to a place we cannot explain and who in their right mind can live in bliss;

or we could say the bones,

if we could forget the skeleton hanging in the classroom corner, its parts needing to be named for the test; if we could put the Halloween decorations—the black-and-white cardboard cutouts, the costumes asking for candy, and the tangled mess suspended from the tree—out of our minds; if we could refuse to work our fingers to bone;

so that we might think of a deep structure that holds everything in place, shaping us, restricting how we might bend, keeping us under control, until it breaks, allowing an arm to dangle how it never had before, a leg to swing as if unattached, a shoulder to rotate beyond its limits; of course, everything must be arranged again, some order found, but we can believe that if only Humpty Dumpty had been put back together again, he would have, carrying the wisdom of his fall, been better than ever before;

those invisible bones know that the hip bone, despite what that silly song teaches us, is not connected to the leg bone but to another hip bone, which proves that connection doesn't just happen but is the result of losing enough of our self-consciousness to shake it all about;

make no bones about it, we mustn't be boneheaded about this or we will find ourselves bone dry, unable to feel it in our bones; then we would have a bone to pick, then the crossbones, waiting underneath the skull, would not be far behind;

we must follow our spine since its curvature will lead us to all connecting points; we must remember that the marrow is essential for our health; we must locate the wishbone without any desire to pull it apart but to hold it in that perpetual moment before its promise is decided;

or we could say the breath,

the in and out of it all, seemingly mundane but amazing, the transformation, the replenishment, the fundamental;

the sweet-and-sour breath that is shared, that enters between thoughts, that lingers after all is said and done, which is to say that such breath breathes beyond words and actions (although it is often their motive), floating into the unseen, gasping at the seen, but never short of breath;

instead, the breath that takes our breath away, the breath we are always trying to catch, inhaling, exhaling until we can only speak under it, in whispers, not knowing how we became breathless;

or we could say the eye,

> the quizzical eye that lives in the instant before it meets the microscope, open, ready to see what is there, eager and resourceful as an intern;

> that sweet eye, accepting as an old monk who has learned the pleasure of watching the mosquito take his blood, embraces what it meets, takes it all in, warming it by its attention—such an eye does not impose its will, its beliefs, its values; no, it gives birth to the moment and lives just for the chance of seeing;

> that consuming eye that comes eyeball to eyeball as an eyewitness, eye-ing everything, everywhere, until what it sees it knows like its own heart (see above);

> that comic eye, crossing over, nosing around;

> that blind eye, smitten, that allows us to see, lidless, staring through the dark, determined to get everything in focus, despite the pain, despite the torn retina, despite the missing pupil (the pupil, of course, is nothing more than the tiny image one sees of oneself reflected in someone else's eye), determined to make its steady look an eye-opener, determined to eliminate the blind spots so that our hard gaze might give way to our wide-eyed perspectives and our wide-eyed perspectives might collapse into our shared vision;

or we could say the ear,

> since the ear, as any artist knows, is on the same plane as the eye, since the ear is never far behind the eye, since the ear confirms the eye as much as the eye confirms the ear, since there is no stopping the ear (it always does its nervous work), since the ear will not be plugged, and since the ear awaits its ache;

> so let's hear it for the ear, that intricate ear, with its hammer and drum, that vibrates into life as it earmarks the deep tones, the pure pitch, and the infectious inflections;

> that inner ear keeps us in balance, stops the stumbles and falls of our poor equilibrium as it holds and molds sounds as if life depended upon it (and it does, for without an earful, we do not grow; without the reverberations

of our words, we weaken; without the monotones of our mantras, there can be no calm); that ear makes us into earwitnesses, insisting we can always be within earshot, can always hear it all, can always take it all in, if only we are willing to move a little closer;

that attentive ear lives on its ear, irritated, stops the quick slide, the in one side and out the other, and puts us up to our ears so that we cannot turn a deaf ear to anyone;

that straining ear that tilts in, presses against the fourth wall, listens in the dark because it is hard to hear for the hard of hearing, for the hard of heart, for the hard;

or we could say the tongue,

that remembers its first French kiss in all its startled sensuousness;

such a tongue knows the necessity of tasting what the eye might miss (the difference, for instance, between salt and sugar), knows when to bite itself (not everything can or should be chewed), and still understands how to appreciate everything that is put before it (a feast is made from its parts);

such a tongue, pierced, accepts its pain so that another might receive its pleasure;

such a tongue is never tongue tied; it licks life, sometimes playing with the cheek, sometimes hurrying to its tip, but always seeking its groove.

or we could say the skin,

shedding its outer layer to allow for growth, casting off its dried-up husk to eschew protection, and exposing a softer self, in fact, so soft, so permeable that one could come to know how love was born;

the pale and dark skin, slipping behind the eyes that watch it touch, knows the politics behind the slogans, behind the legislative fist, behind difference; that scary skin, like white fungus, eats away;

hairy skin, unplucked, aping us, telling us where we are and where we've been;

carved skin, perhaps so cracked and creviced that its lines tell of its fortune; perhaps so wrinkled and worn that its firmest shape comes only when pressed; perhaps so malleable that its contours take form only in another's grip; perhaps so aged that it simply resists its return to the bone, refusing to be any longer the bones' clothes;

skinned skin, revealing not what is hidden but its thickness, its toughness, its torment, forming a scab that itches (don't pick), crusting into brown-and-black palimpsests (don't pick) that are historical markers (all histories, of course, can be picked apart to uncover what is underneath; there are incidents that happen that we must account for and that account of us), tattooed;

grafted skin, layer on layer, taken, over and over, from the skin of one's teeth, from what is under one's skin, from what irritates like a splinter; skin that is willing to touch, so gently, oh so gently, it learns to speak desire;

oiled skin, slippery, ready for the wisdom of coalescence, of body pressed to body, of the unspeakable joy, the unspeakable life.

Part II—The Playful Body: Fragments Circling an Argument

1

I speak the heart's discourse because the heart is never far from what matters. Without the heart pumping its words, we are nothing but an outdated dictionary, untouched.

2

Whenever we engage in research, we are offering a first-person narrative. Even our most traditional work is someone's story. Notice:

> *Review of the Literature*: I had been reading about this subject for a long time now. Working through this reading, I realized that I might classify it into several categories. After doing that, I saw that there were still several questions unanswered.
> *Research Question*: I really wanted to know what was going on with this unexplored area.

Procedure: So I decided that I would collect some information on the subject. I gathered together a bunch of people, people of various types and from various places, and I asked them about my question.

Results: I added up all their responses, did a few calculations, and their responses were just what I guessed what they would be.

Interpretation: I can explain what everyone said lots of different ways, but I believe this one way makes the most sense. I have lots more questions to ask, but I sure feel better now that I have an answer to my question.

3

Some would object: "To say all research is a first-person narrative is not to say that all research is about the heart. The heart pushes the self forward to places it doesn't belong."

And I would respond: "I don't want to go places where the heart is not welcome. Such places frighten me."

"Are you frightened by the truth?" would come the rejoinder.

"No, I'm frightened by what poses as the truth."

4

There are two kinds of truth: The first believes in "is." It finds comfort in the equation. The second, as any poet knows, lets "is" stand in until a better verb can be found. It finds joy in fracturing the infinitive "to be." The first is useful for building bridges; the second for building people.

5

Still troubled, some would continue: "There are things that just should not be shared."

And I would ask: "What of the human condition should be kept hidden?"

"Research is not therapy! It is not a narcissistic display!"

"What harm could come from using the self to display what might be therapeutic? Who benefits from such hidings? Why must we work under an epistemology of 'not that?'"

6

The heart has its followers: Banks and Banks, Behar, Clifford and Marcus; Denzin, Denzin and Lincoln, Ellis, Ellis and Bochner, Bochner and Ellis,

Gingrich-Philbrook, Goodall, Holman Jones, Jones, Lockford, Miller and Pelias, Madison, Pineau, Pollock, Richardson, Rushing and Frentz, Spry, Stoller, Tillmann-Healy, Trinh, and many, many others. In their most impassioned moments, they believe with Ruth Behar that scholarship that "doesn't break your heart just isn't worth doing anymore" (177).

7

The heart has its opponents: Atkinson, Burgoon, Craig, Shields, Parks, Wendt, and many, many others. In their most impassioned moments, they believe with Parks that there are limits to what should count as scholarship. They are gatekeepers guarding the boundaries of their disciplines.

8

To represent the human anatomy without including the heart is the equivalent of describing a car without mentioning its motor. The crisis in representation stems from forgetting where the power is.

Pinning a butterfly to a mat, classifying it, and presenting it to other collectors says nothing of its beauty. It's always a question of what story you want to tell.

Knowing what is true, what is valid and reliable, and what to predict should come from listening to as many stories as you can and deciding how to act responsibly.

9

Science is the act of looking at a tree and seeing lumber. Poetry is the act of looking at a tree and seeing a tree.

The alchemy that separates the head from the heart finds no gold.

10

The body protects the heart with its bones. Each notch on the spinal cord is a philosophical presupposition, each rib a theoretical stance. The pelvis is the foundation of practice.

11

All the talk about "the body" forgets that its importance rests in the fact that it exists in "a body," a body with a heart. As Adrienne Rich explains:

Perhaps we need a moratorium on saying "the body." For it's also possible to abstract "the" body. When I write "the body," I see nothing in particular. To write "my body" plunges me into lived experience, particularly: I see scars, disfigurements, discolorations, damages, losses, as well as what pleases me. . . . To say "the body" lifts me away from what has given me primary perspective. To say "my body" reduces the temptation to grandiose assertions. (67)

And for those who may still be tempted by the grandiose, it useful to remember with Gingrich-Philbrook that one's body might misguide, deceive, or lie, that one's body might be ideologically suspect.

12

A heart finds its vocabulary in the senses. It wants a "sensuous scholarship," "a mixing of head and heart" (Stoller, xviii). Instead of a "bloodless prose that saps the body of its sensuousness" (xv), it wants its poem. It wants to be set free.

Part III—The Ready Body: Moving Forward with Heart
The Heart's Scene

The essays in this book come together at a time of crises—a crisis of representation and a crisis of faith. The crisis of representation has been well documented and discussed. Many scholars have come to understand that what they believed to be claims of truth were best understood as demonstrations of the inadequacy of language or as reflections of their own point of view and political interests. As such ideas took hold, their certainty peeled away from the academic tower like dead ivy. They felt nervous, shaken, unsure when or how to speak.

The crisis of faith appeared in academic circles when a growing number of faculty discovered that the university life was not what they expected or bargained for. They were teaching students who seemed more interested in grades than learning. They were working for administrators who seemed more concerned with the bottom line than quality education. They were going to endless meetings that didn't seem to matter, writing meaningless reports that seemed to disappear into the bureaucracy, and learning that service seemed to have little effect on others' lives. Productivity was the motto of the day, so they published article after article that no one seemed to read, particularly those who were the focus of the study. They wrote piece after piece on social issues, but none seemed to make any difference. They researched topics that got them promotions and tenure but seemed removed from who they were. They felt empty, despondent, disillusioned. They felt spiritually and ethically bankrupt.

Then some scholars began to recognize that the emperor and, for that matter, they themselves were wearing no clothes. They started to question why university life had to be that way, why they had to be removed from their work, why only certain forms of discourse counted as knowledge, why they didn't feel more connected to those they studied, why their mind should be split from their body, why they had to keep their emotions in check, why they could not speak from the heart.

The Heart's Genres

Some of the included essays are autoethnographic, in search of the nexus of self and culture. They show a self maneuvering through time and space to reveal how cultural logics enable and constraint. They seek a resonance.

Some are autobiographical, a self struggling to understand, a self constructing an identity. Turn the page and find another self. Turn the page and find the contradictions. Turn the page and watch the self slip away. They see the self as a springboard, as a witness.

Some are performative, playful, longing toward poem. They believe in words. They want to language a stone. They have the jitters. Their heart beats in a phrase.

Some are scholarly musings, asking what do we need to know next, what is not exhausted, what is still of interest. Their arguments march to old drums. Their flags are well known. They are trying to teach. Beware.

Some are creative nonfiction, certain that they can only name by way of the poem. They dance with the facts.

Some are personal narratives, stories to share because they are meaningful beyond any teller. They often tell more than they should. They seek connection. They are listening for your answer.

Some are memoirs, remembrances of days past that take over today's presence. They cannot be put away, buried. They want air.

Some are prayers in search of gods. They refuse to stop believing. They will not be silent. They live under the skin. They are searching for answers.

All are methodological calls, writings that mark a different space. They collect in the body: an ache, a fist, a soup. They ask for your consideration.

The Heart's Procedure

Genre encourages procedure by setting expectancies in place. Writers and readers understand that to call forward a form is to signal that certain tactics will be deployed. Some generic forms privilege argument, logic, and facts; others privilege life's passions, puzzles, and possibilities. The essays in this book, always reaching for the heart's discourse, play out their generic potential by striving first and foremost for the latter rather than the former, although the two orientations are never completely separate. To pursue life's passions, puzzles, and possibilities, writers and readers benefit from a close association with a scholarship that is evocative, multifaceted, reflexive, empathic, and useful.

Evocative scholarship has language doing its hardest work, finding its most telling voice, and revealing its deepest secrets. It is literature that makes its writer and readers take notice not just of its points but also of its aesthetic presentation. Often it relies on the figurative and rests on form. It avoids the cliché, the familiar. It depends upon the creative and finds its force in the imaginative.

Multifaceted scholarship turns and twists, stands to all sides, considers; it looks under and over, searches from top to bottom, ponders; it walks around, digs into, and tunnels through before it acknowledges that it can never see it all. It never stops trying, even though it may elect to speak from one stance at any given moment, even though it knows that to speak is to always be located in history, to always be positioned and partisan.

Reflexive scholarship comes back around, points to itself in order to say this is where it stands, at least at this moment, with these qualifiers and with these questions. It hopes to make the declarative duck, to shake the seemingly unshakable, and to feel the answer squirm. It lives for maybe.

Empathic scholarship connects person to person in the belief in a shared and complex world. While it recognizes that no two lives are identical, it celebrates when one says to another, "Me too." It welcomes identification, the witnessing of commonality, as well as separation, the claim of difference. Both require a taking in, a knowing and a feeling.

Useful scholarship reaches toward an audience. It cares. It wants to make a difference when speaking to members of the scholarly community and to those under study. It enters the ongoing discussion only after it has done its work. It knows what has been said. It works in behalf of social justice. It is a cultural laborer.

The Heart's Desire

The essays that follow tell stories of my daily life at home and in the academy. I share them not because they seem extraordinary but because they seem ordinary, unremarkable, except that they are like others' tales; not all others, but familiar enough, I hope, to find commonality with many people. They want to open a space of identification, a place of understanding. They strive to connect heart to heart. I also share them as examples of alternative methodological possibilities for generating research. As implied above, they participate in the ongoing discussions of what constitutes acceptable scholarship. They request entry into the academic arena. For some, this request will seem unnecessary; for others, it will seem inappropriate to even ask. Regardless, I hold close to my heart the delightful fantasy that the essays will be met with critical compassion. So, dear readers, come forward with open hearts and minds, ready to feel what might be there and ready to think of its possibilities; ready to accept and ready to reject; ready to pull in and ready to push away.

The Heart's Thanks

I start with the wonderful colleagues in performance studies I work with at Southern Illinois University, Carbondale: Craig Gingrich-Philbrook, Jonny Gray, Elyse Pineau, and Nathan Stucky. To them, I owe immeasurable gratitude. They are my daily co-authors. Likewise, to Sheron Dailey (Indiana State University), Carolyn Ellis (University of South Florida), Lee Jenkins (San Francisco State University), Lesa Lockford (Bowling Green State University), Mary Hinchcliff-Pelias (Southern Illinois University), H. L. Goodall (University of North Carolina, Greensboro), and Tessa O. Pelias (University of Illinois), I can only say that your presence is a part of every page. Thanks for being there.

I would also like to thank the people at AltaMira Press, particularly Mitch Allen, Becca Smith, Michael Marino, and Kate Babbitt.

Finally, I would like to acknowledge several publishers for permission to reprint the following essays:

"Organizational Performance: Playing the Field." *Journal of the Association for Communication Administration* 10 (1994): 128–34, co-authored with Elyse Pineau. Reprinted by permission of the National Communication Association.

"Always Dying: Living between *Da* and *Fort*." *Qualitative Inquiry* 6 (2000): 229–37. Reprinted by permission of Sage Publications.

"The Critical Life." *Communication Education* 49 (2000): 220–28. Reprinted by permission of Taylor and Francis.

"The Academic Tourist." *Qualitative Inquiry* 9 (2001): 369–73. Reprinted by permission of Sage Publications.

"For Father and Son: An Ethnodrama With No Catharsis." *Ethnographically Speaking*. Ed. Arthur P. Bochner and Carolyn Ellis, 35–43. Walnut Creek, CA: AltaMira, 2002. Reprinted by permission of Rowman & Littlefield.

"Carolyn Ellis: Helplessly Attached to Being Human." *American Communication Journal* 6. Available online at http://www.acjournal.org. Reprinted by permission of the American Communication Association.

Works Cited

Atkinson, P. "Narrative Turn in a Blind Alley?" *Qualitative Health Research* 7 (1997): 325–44.

Banks, Anna, and Stephen P. Banks, eds. *Fiction and Social Research: By Ice or Fire.* Walnut Creek, CA: AltaMira, 1998.

Behar, Ruth. *The Vulnerable Observer: Anthropology That Breaks Your Heart.* Boston: Beacon, 1996.

Bochner, Arthur P., and Carolyn Ellis, eds. *Ethnographically Speaking: Autoethnography, Literature, and Aesthetics.* Walnut Creek, CA: AltaMira, 2002.

Burgoon, Michael. "Instruction About Communication: On Divorcing Dame Speech." *Communication Education* 68 (1993): 97–105.

Clifford, James, and George E. Marcus, eds. *Writing Culture: The Poetics and Politics of Ethnography.* Berkeley and Los Angeles: University of California Press, 1986.

Craig, Robert T. "Textual Harassment." *American Communication Journal* 1, no. 2 (1998). Available online at http://acjournal.org/holdings/vol1/Iss2/special/craig.htm.

Denzin, Norman K. *Interpretive Ethnography: Ethnographic Practices for the Twenty-First Century.* Thousand Oaks, CA: Sage, 1997.

Denzin, Norman K., and Yvonna S. Lincoln, eds. *Handbook of Qualitative Research.* 2d ed. Thousand Oaks, CA: Sage, 2000.

Ellis, Carolyn. *Final Negotiations: A Story of Love, Loss, and Chronic Illness.* Philadelphia: Temple University Press, 1995.

Ellis, Carolyn, and Arthur P. Bochner, eds. *Composing Ethnography: Alternative Forms of Qualitative Writing.* Walnut Creek, CA: AltaMira, 1996.

Gingrich-Philbrook, Craig. "What I 'Know' about the Story (for those about to tell personal narratives on stage)." *The Future of Performance Studies: Visions and Revisions.* Ed. Sheron J. Dailey, 298–300. Annandale, VA: National Communication Association, 1998.

———. "Bite Your Tongue: Four Songs of Body and Language." *The Green Window: Proceeding of the Giant City Conference on Performative Writing,* 1–7. Eds. Lynn C. Miller and Ronald J. Pelias. Carbondale, IL: Southern Illinois University, 2001.

Goodall, H. L., Jr. *Casing the Promised Land: The Autobiography of an Organizational Detective as Cultural Ethnographer.* Carbondale, IL: Southern Illinois University Press, 1989.

———. *Living in the Rock 'n' Roll Mystery: Reading Context, Self, and Other as Clues.* Carbondale, IL: Southern Illinois University Press, 1991.

———. *Divine Signs: Connecting Spirit to Community.* Carbondale, IL: Southern Illinois University Press, 1996.

———. *Writing the New Ethnography.* Walnut Creek, CA.: AltaMira, 2000.

Holman Jones, Stacy. *Kaleidoscope Notes: Writing Women's Music and Organizational Culture.* Walnut Creek, CA: AltaMira, 1998.

Jones, Joni L. "*sista docta*: Performance as Critique of the Academy." *The Drama Review* 41 (1997): 51–67.

Lockford, Lesa. *Performing Femininity*. Walnut Creek, CA: AltaMira, in press.

Miller, Lynn C., and Ronald J. Pelias, eds. *The Green Window: Proceedings of the Giant City Conference on Performative Writing*. Carbondale, IL: Southern Illinois University, 2001.

Madison, D. Soyini. "Performing Theory/Embodied Writing." *Text and Performance Quarterly* 19 (1999): 107–24.

Parks, Malcolm R. "Where Does Scholarship Begin?" *American Communication Journal* 1, no. 2 (1998). Available online at http://acjournal.org/holdings/vol1/Iss2/special/parks.htm.

Pineau, Elyse. "Nursing Mother and Articulating Absence." *Text and Performance Quarterly* 20 (2000): 1–19.

Pollock, Della. *Telling Bodies Performing Birth*. New York: Columbia University Press, 1999.

Rich, Adrienne. *Arts of the Possible*. New York: W. W. Norton, 2001.

Richardson. Laurel. *Fields of Play: Constructing an Academic Life*. New Brunswick, NJ: Rutgers University Press, 1997.

Rushing, Janice Hocker, and Thomas S. Frentz. "The Gods Must Be Crazy: The Denial of Descent in Academic Scholarship." *Quarterly Journal of Speech* 85 (1999): 229–46.

Shields, Donald C. "Symbolic Convergence and Speech Communication Theories: Sensing and Examining Dis/Enchantment with the Theoretical Robustness of Critical Autoethnography." *Communication Monographs* 67 (2000): 392–421.

Spry, Tami. "Performing Autoethnography: An Embodied Methodological Praxis." *Qualitative Inquiry* 7 (2001): 706–32.

Stoller, Paul. *Sensuous Scholarship*. Philadelphia: University of Pennsylvania Press, 1997.

Tillmann-Healy, Lisa M. *Between Gay and Straight: Understanding Friendship across Sexual Orientation*. Walnut Creek, CA: AltaMira, 2001.

Trinh, T. Minh-ha. *Woman, Native, Other: Writing Postcoloniality and Feminism*. Bloomington: Indiana University Press, 1989.

Wendt, Ted A. "The Ways and Means of Knowing: The 'Problem' of Scholarship in a Postmodern World." *American Communication Journal* 1, no. 2 (1998). Available online at http://acjournal.org/holdings/vol1/Iss2/special/wendt.htm.

CHAPTER 2

A Personal Ecology

Biology and biography come together like sperm to egg to begin in place, to find its attachment, to claim its region. The egg and sperm that coalesced to form the genetic imprint called Ron entered the world July 18, 1946, in a town that sits below sea level known as New Orleans, or N'awlins for those who live there. This crescent city, this city of canals and levees, of the Mississippi River and Lake Pontchartrain, of swamps and crawfish, cradles itself just above water. I splashed on the scene as the second of three children to a Greek father, a wholesale grocer by trade, who had, from the perspective of other Greeks, the poor judgment to marry my German mother and produce three children who did not speak Greek. Instead, we spoke N'awlins.

We did not speak the N'awlins of the Yats, those other people who got their name from the question, "Where are you at?" meaning, of course, "How are you doing?" which should not be confused with "Hw's ya Mom 'n 'em?" meaning, of course, "How is your mother and the others in your family?" No, we spoke the N'awlins of the Lake Shore, a N'awlins that was made from dredging the lake to make more land, land above sea level, higher than the rest of the city so that when floods came, the water would simply pass on to other neighborhoods, would pass on to the Yats.

During the summers of my teen years, I would drive with my dad from our Lake Shore neighborhood to the place of his work, Jackson Wholesale Grocery on Decatur Street in the French Quarter, a place where he would park illegally, having made the necessary arrangements with the police. He would park in the shadow and smell of Jax Brewery, that beige building belching hops that had swallowed the two blocks directly across from his place of business. It was here that I would learn my first lessons of work.

I would learn from my Uncle Jimmy that every day after our trucks were loaded for delivery, we deserved a tour of the Jax Brewery. I would learn from him too that whenever the Duck Lady would approach, work must stop so that he could give her a hug. I was told that the Duck Lady, who resembled a duck to such an extent that she was able to make her living by walking the French Quarter with a duck on a leash and selling caricatures of herself, must always be treated like a queen. "Come here, baby," he would say, "give old Jimmy some sugar."

I would learn from the loaders and drivers of trucks that I did not want to load and drive trucks. Sweating in the N'awlins' sun, sweating under the fumes of the passing cars and trucks, sweating under the scrutinizing eyes of the other workers as they watch how the boss's son would be treated, I would learn the weight of canned goods and the bulk of paper goods. Day in and day out, dirt demanded its design. But I knew that, unlike the men who worked beside me in the loading bay, I could escape back to the Lake Shore. I could wash away the day as if it were an experiment, an initiation rite before I would cross over to my place, my place with my father.

I would learn from my father by watching him work, for he was a worker of words. He worked words as he made his rounds, writing up orders from the small corner grocery stores run by Italians, Koreans, and Jews, by Cubans, Puerto Ricans, and Chinese, by Blacks, Germans, and Russians. That Greek man would imitate them all, taking on their accents, and would convince them all that they needed another case of Libby's canned carrots. He worked words when he worked his workers, sometimes joking and laughing, sometimes cursing and yelling, and sometimes praising and hugging. He worked words when he worked me, slowly, over the years to believe that my place was with him. His words were maps of the Big Easy, the place he called his own, charting all the river's curves. His words were tour books pointing out places of pleasure we could share. His words were street signs telling me where I wanted to go. His words were poems for father and son. I would listen and I would learn to enter his Lake Shore world, his house above sea level, his place of privilege where our biology and biography became one.

So here I am trying to share my ecological identity, trying to show how this living organism moves in a particular place with other living organism. I am here trying to see the drama of it all, trying to look with a performative eye. At first, I thought I would just do a performance: I saw a stage filled with lecterns. I would project slides of the homes where I have lived, the offices where I have worked, and the theatres where I have performed. After each slide, I would say, "Nice, uh?" Then I'd begin to describe the slide, but shortly after I would start, a voice on tape would intrude: "Sorry, your time is up." I would then move to another lectern, to begin in another place with another slide, only to be interrupted again. The process would continue, for I have long known that time does not leave space alone.

But it was a performance I could not do when I remembered the house on Milan Street, the house before the one on Lake Shore. It was large three-story in desperate need of paint shared by three families, mine squeezed into the middle. It was a house where we did not fit, a house of noises coming from above and below, always the yelling, the crying, and the police, with whom my Dad could not make the necessary arrangements, pounding on the door. It was the house that, every Tuesday night, hosted my grandparents who spoke only Greek while my Mother sat in silence. The large oak in the front of the house, the one I would climb to escape the noise, was cut down before it did any structural damage. It is the house my brother, the architect, just bought and renovated. He painted it bright red. Now he and his wife live on all three floors.

I want us to soar across this page like the bateleur eagle does the sky, turning somersaults and clapping our wings in midair before we dive screaming toward the ground. For this is our beginning.

I want us to create, like the bullfrog, sounds through our ears so that what we have to say will mix with what we hear from each other. For this is a mating call.

I want us to pull each other in like the alligator snapping turtle who uses a small, worm-shaped growth at the base of its mouth as a lure. For this is our seduction of one another.

I want us to feed each other, like falcons who pass food while in flight. For this can only be done together.

I want us like basilisk lizards of Central America to run across water. For this asks us to do the impossible.

I want us to speak as loudly as the blue whale, whose sounds have been measured at a million times more intense than a jet plane, so that all might hear the alarm. For this is the time and place to act.

I want us, like the anteater, to have spikes on our tongues. For this is the tongue's stinging and saving tale.

I want us, like the warthog, to get down on our knees to eat. For this is a humble act, a prayer as we feast at the altar.

I want us to be as unnoticeable as the bee hummingbird, the smallest warm-blooded animal in the world. For this is not about us, but without us, there are no others.

This large warm-blooded animal measures his worth as he moves from place to place by what he takes and by what he leaves behind. My first move was to Dallas, where I learned, to my surprise, that I had a N'awlins accent. I would say, introducing myself, "I'm Ron Pelias from N'awlins," and they would say, "You're who from where?" It was in Dallas that I took my first linguistic steps away from my place of birth. It was in Dallas too that I first found others to love who were not from my place of birth. I married a Missouri woman who grew up on a farm trying to be the son her father needed after her brother's death. Although we never lived on that farm, she never left it.

I left her behind on that Missouri farm with my two-week-old son when I went from Dallas to Vietnam, from higher education to a lower education, lower than the holes our B-52's made when they dropped their loads, lower than the sandbag shelters we built to protect us from the rockets, lower than I would crawl when the fighting would start. I was a medic patching wounds of the body and of the mind. I worked in the area that the army called "mental hygiene." My job was to floss brains so that they might go out once again into the field. When I brought my flossed brain back home, I had changed, and my wife decided to stay on that Missouri farm with her new lover and my year-old son.

I put myself in another place. I went for more education of the higher kind to a city called Urbana. My hope was to become more urbane. I wanted to learn how to move within the academic world with some savvy. Instead, I learned that savvy is a sorry facade. I learned what Marvin Bell meant when he said, "As for me, I know nothing. But do not think one can know nothing so easily. It has taken me many years" (224). I have learned the irony of ignorance. And I have taken that ignorance to the places where I have taught— Blacksburg, Detroit, Carbondale—and watched it grow each time I entered a classroom, each time I read a book, each time I thought I had an answer. Now, fully converted, I am ignorance's preacher.

As I preach ignorance, I am mobile. Moving from location to location, I am repositioning myself, changing who is present. Scholars are cited and then left behind; students are taught and then left behind; politicians are applauded and then left behind. Friends too are no longer present: Bill and Tom from Dallas are gone; Tony and Cheryl from Blacksburg are gone; Mary and Steve from Urbana are gone; Claire and Larry from Detroit are gone. And now that I am unsettled in Carbondale, others leave me. I know with Mark Strand the difficulty of "Keeping Things Whole":

When I walk
I part the air
and always
the air moves in
to fill the spaces
where my body's been. (10)

I travel twice a year to N'awlins, to the comforts of home, to the place of my making. When I'm there, I speak N'awlins.

Have you ever noticed that all the programs on the Nature Channel have the same plot? They start with a panorama of some unfamiliar place, perhaps in South America or Africa, before slowly moving in for the close-up. We see the animals' habitats, their mating rituals, their births, their hunting (necessary for feeding their young), and their migratory paths. Then we see them as the hunted. Sometimes they escape; sometimes they are caught and eaten. The camera pulls away and we are told how life goes on along the Amazon or the Nile. And as I watch in fascination, my mind always wanders to the people who hide themselves along the Amazon and Nile so that they might make these films. I think of their sacrifice, their active stillness, their hushed speech.

As a tourist of a different kind, I frequent resorts: swimming pools with waterfalls next to open bars, green golf courses manicured by migrant work-ers, and rooms, cleaned daily, overlooking the ocean. I see Europe in twenty-one days without ever having to carry my bags or to speak anything but English. I travel to conventions—New York, Chicago, San Francisco, Atlanta, San Diego, Boston—paying over a $100 a night for a room, not to mention plane fare and $12 hamburgers, so that I might listen to others like me. When the time comes, I am ready to be home, ready to return to my routines, and ready to hear Guy Debord's words: "Tourism is the chance to go and see what has been made trite" (120).

But I will travel again. I remember a family trip to London where we went to all the major sites—Big Ben, the Tower Bridge, the British Museum, Buckingham Palace. My twelve-year-old daughter, though, only wanted to watch the street performers by Covent Garden. She liked how they could gather a crowd, how they could make the crowd laugh, how they might pull her on stage. She wanted to have everyone's eyes on her, the eyes of those who were delaying lunch to see her, eyes of those who were hiding behind the shoul-ders of others, the eyes of those who stood in silence, hushed by the drama of it all. She knows how to get picked from the crowd. She knows it's all a mat-ter of where you stand.

Have you ever noticed that the plots in all theatre are just like the ones on the Nature Channel?

They come when the food is put out. The bullying grackles come in groups and take the closest spots. In between, the sparrows slip in. When the nasty blue jays arrive, everyone moves out of the way. The cardinals make their appearances in pairs. The cedar waxwings prefer the feeder down the block. The juncos are selective; they study the situation and come only so often. The wrens are always too eager, and the chickadees are always too cautious. The mockingbirds, above it all, seem to have an opinion about everything that is going on. Only one indigo bunting has ever come. The killdeer never bother; they're too busy scurrying around. The mourning doves settle in for it all.

Scientists have recently discovered through genetic testing that birds are not as faithful as they once thought. Walter Piper, a biology professor from George Mason University, is quoted in the newspaper as saying, "Initially we thought birds were largely monogamous. That was in the pre-molecular era. Then suddenly we were all appalled, some of us at least, to learn there's a lot of hanky-panky going on." Robins were found to be particularly promiscuous. Songbird after songbird was proven unfaithful.

I had a dream that I was going with some students to Sauk Valley Community College, near the birthplace of Ronald Reagan, for the nourishment that a performance festival can provide. We were driving along when our van just seemed to stop. We eased it to the side of road. As we stood there trying to figure out what we should do, we heard them—softly, at first, then louder. They were approaching us—Republicans, spewing Bible verses, moving forward like people from *Night of the Living Dead*. Falwell was there saying that Tinky Winky was a gay role model for the two-and-under set. They surrounded us. We got in the van and locked the doors. They came closer. They broke in the windows. They pulled us one by one from the van, beating us with their good intentions. They droned, over and over again, "You are one of us." I was scared. As King James was coming toward my head, I awoke in a sweat, glad I was home. Still shaking, I remembered James Clifford's words: Location "is an itinerary rather than a bounded site—a series of encounters and translations" (11).

So I am home and I must decide what I should do. I will speak my N'awlins patois, for I have no other choice. I am located. But to what end? I try to walk upon this earth doing more good than harm. I try in the classes I teach and in the shows I direct to create a healthy ecological space. I try to know what is good for our environment. But my actions are always pollutants and our resources are never replenishable. There is never enough time; there are never enough places. Even so, you will find me at home, pulling things from my "wherehouse," trying to speak of new times, of new places, struggling to find our nature.

Works Cited

Bell, Marvin. *A Marvin Bell Reader: Selected Poetry and Prose*. Hanover, NH: Middlebury College Press, 1994.

Clifford, James. *Routes: Travel and Translation in the Late Twentieth Century*. Cambridge, MA: Harvard University Press, 1997.

Debord, Guy. *The Society of the Spectacle*. Trans. Donald Nicholson-Smith. New York: Zone Books, 1995.

Strand, Mark. "Keeping Things Whole." *Selected Poems*. New York: Alfred A. Knopf, 1990.

CHAPTER 3

The Body's Complaint

The Hangnail

Split, on the edge, pointed, hanging on, rooted, calling to the thumb to rub its irritation before the teeth, turning this way and that, struggle to pull it away. Bitten in half, it swells, reddens, squats down. Perhaps a little blood runs around the cuticle; perhaps a little pus oozes when pushed. It awaits further action—the silver clippers, the curved scissors—in its two-day-long war that it never wins.

The Runny Nose

Always already running, running, and running, with the help of a little blow or just on its own, running just because, running through Kleenex, running down the throat, running down the lip, running, running faster and faster, dripping and drenching until the watered proboscis flowers red.

The Smashed Finger

Unexpected, sudden as a quake, shaking, until the fingers of the opposite hand stop the flapping. Squeezed secure, the dance of the ows begins and then, because the eyes must see, damage is assessed: skin ripped, nail destroyed, debris. Throbbing through the cleaning cool water and salve, wrapped in white, and taped into obedience, it considers its stupidity.

The Bruised Thigh

Beckoning black, blue, and even a bit of green and spreading like a small spill, it forgets its origin. Perhaps it was a turn into a table, perhaps a slip against a car, perhaps a partner's knee during the night. After asserting its tender presence, it leaves without a trace, without a second thought.

The Upset Stomach

Burning from favorite foods, from vicious viruses, or from deadly demands, burning from acids that know what it is willing to have around, burning from the pleasure of producing fire, it remembers its beginnings and its endings. It refuses to stay put. Alka-Seltzer, Titralac, and Milk of Magnesia seek the symptom and forget the cause. Upset, it returns.

The Athlete's Foot

As if it meant one was accomplished in anything but producing putrid skin, that rotten white layer covering the itch. As if it meant one could attend to the game without scratching, without wanting to pull that sweatsock, back and forth, between the toes until relief comes, without wondering how such a visitor got into one's arena. As if it meant one knew how to pick sides.

The Stubbed Toe

Quick as a moment's neglect, sharp, on the sofa's edge, sharp, on the chair's leg, sharp, on the bed's frame, shooting up, speeding to the brain to complain, and then, while you hop, grab hold, and try to see the damage, the brain decides that nothing is wrong any longer.

The Headache

First comes location—the back of the head, the forehead, the temples—location is everything. If you want to do it right, location is the key. Then decide upon the degree—the mild, the moderate, the monstrous—each calls for more or less work on your part. You must be up to the task. Finally, watch out for the cures—a pause to rub, medication, bed—they'll take you down, make you think you don't matter. Remember, you can rule the day.

The Ingrown Toenail

Turned in on itself, yellowing, it is tuned in to the frequency of each step, triggering the same sad signal, announcing and lamenting its crooked ways. Only the knife or its own will can alter the course of its extravagance.

The Scraped Knee

A layer here, a layer there—it doesn't much matter until there is blood. Then you've got something, a scab to be picked and picked again for the blood, red, coming to the surface, coming up like hot springs, warm, bubbling, bubbling beyond its borders into a slow trickle, down, down the leg, a river of no regrets that hardens into today's map.

The Abscessed Tooth

A finger, pushing down hard, finds the spot where pressure gives some momentary relief until the mouth fills with sourness, until the chair tilts back and other fingers begin to work, probing, clasping, and pulling, until blood and spit swirl around porcelain and the tongue snakes into emptiness.

The Busted Lip

Swollen into a protruding pout, the puffy fat hangs like rotting fruit, discolored, never to be placed next to its own kind, never to be touched, never to be painted. Cracked, dried skin, blackened on the edges, pleads for absolution.

The Stiff Neck

Rolling first to the left and then to the right, the head pulls against habit and desire. Muscles tighten until turning becomes a trick. There is no moving without stiffness, no eating without spills, no speaking without strain. The bed accepts, but does not welcome, the calcified, calculating body.

The Itchy Anus

There is nothing to do but to wash, wash away the pulling hairs, the sticky mess, the brown streak, wash until all that is left has been rubbed raw, wash until there is no need to prod, to poke, to loosen, wash until the soreness can be flushed away. Then, pat dry and powder, remembering previous times.

The Broken Leg

Even bracing against impact, the bone broke beyond the skin. Put back in place, the leg regrets its weight. Over time, the cast, marked with faded best wishes, conceals the itch. Hobbling on crutches, you clasp the coat hanger and then sit and scratch, scratching away at the irrepressible and the irretrievable.

The Arthritic Hand

Open and shut, open and shut, the hand, in spite of its wisdom, pulls against itself. Best left alone, best left to its own devices, best left to its slow curl that cups its pain, it surrenders to the lap to rest. Later, the jar, the doorknob, and the steering wheel will have their way. The world is buttoned.

The Scratched Eye

The edge of the plastic float sliced across as you splashed in the pool. Tears tried to soothe you but you squeezed shut, locked against all possibilities. Afraid, you pressed your hand against disbelief. You rubbed against your better judgment. Fighting your reflexes, you force your lids open and you see. You see with a dim blur. After drops, your good eye surveys the damage you've done and ponders life alone. You never saw it coming.

The Twisted Ankle

The sidewalk's edge, the tree's fallen branch, or the rug's rugged seam know how little it takes—a misplaced foot here, a wrong step there—before all tumbles down. Swollen beyond bones, bruised, too weak to support even a broken spirit, it turns to the crutch for its hazardous rescue.

The Sore Back

Not wanting to sit, to bend, or to turn, not wanting to pour a simple cup of coffee, to brush a few teeth, or to wash a little dish, not wanting to whine, one rests on the floor, still and stiff as a door that has fallen from its hinges, or one stands erect, a wide-eyed, frozen sentry frightened by the thought of movement.

The Chest Pains

It's probably gas, indigestion, but you never know. You eat more red meat than you should. You never get enough exercise. Your job is filled with stress. You take a deep breath and try to stay calm. You feel the tightness, the pulling that makes you want to double over. You feel it move into your left arm. You wonder if your fear could cause what you fear.

The Cancerous Throat

From deep below, breath breaks on its last prayer. It is difficult to swallow. Coupled with a little cough, the voice turns grave. Speech is sentenced to silence. And soon that once-smooth connection between head and heart shuts, strangling it all. There are no more complaints.

CHAPTER 4

Speech and the Body's Presence

Speaking of the Body

It is watching, taking everything in. It wants to know what I'm up to, what I will tell. I do know its secrets, but my purpose here is not to tattle or to confess. Instead, I speak the body as it speaks me. I want to delve into my body's workings, not its biology but its autobiology, its autobiography, its autoethnography, particularly as it connects to speech. I come as my body's friend in a desire to explore how it moves me and how I move it in the world and in language. So I speak of the body positioned, possessed, and posed, given the limits of my vested interests, for whatever might come.

Telling the Body's Tale

First, did I mention that I have one, a rather large one? Standing, it measures about 6'3" and weighs about 220 pounds. Its size can frighten, particularly small children. It has rounded shoulders, a balding head, and a full belly. It also has a pleasant enough smile and some agility. Most of the time it does, within its limits, what it's told. As it ages well into its fifties, those limits are changing. It misses running with the unreflective abandon that it once had as a child. It has the anatomy that marks it as male. Its skin is called white, but it really is a light tan, perhaps with a touch of olive pigmentation from its Greek heritage. How it moves through the world also clamors "white male." All of its parts are functioning, some better than others. More often than not, it remains covered, protected from the elements and wisecracks. I keep it with me always.

I can usually trust that it will be well behaved. Only upon rare occasions will it produce unwelcome sounds or propagate unsightly blemishes. Yes, it has allowed drool to run down its chin, food to get stuck between its teeth, and snot to hang from its nose hairs, but such moments are the exception rather than the rule. It doesn't try to embarrass me. There have been situations, of course, when it dozed off at the wrong time, when it failed to perform up to expectations, and when it was inappropriately exposed—nothing indecent, mind you, but little acts of misunderstanding or confusion, like when it erroneously thought the doctor needed its pants dropped in order to get a shot or when it mistakenly walked into the wrong restroom and began its business as it wondered why there were no urinals. Such moments embarrass because, like I said, it is usually well behaved.

I have to admit too that there are situations when it simply decides to be ill. It orders up a little fever, a sinus headache, or indigestion. It never has asked me to confront anything serious but it always threatens such a possibility, and as it ages, it seems to remind me of its power more frequently. This, of course, is just an ongoing issue of who claims to be in charge. Negotiations are part of our daily routine: If I don't eat that donut, will you keep a headache away? If I exercise regularly, will you let the heart continue to beat? If I get annual checkups, will you stop cancer from coming?

Kurt Vonnegut taught me in his 1971 address to the National Institute of Arts and Letters what most people only suspect: "Happiness is chemical." He added, "Before I knew that, I used to investigate happiness by means of questions and answers." Sometimes though, the body's chemicals seem so out of order that its voice and hands shake when speaking. Stage fright, people call it, but it is just a chemical malfunction—too much or too little of this or that. Other times its chemicals are so off that it loses control. Chemicals keep it from speaking in a calm, rational manner, listening without interruption, or holding steady what it needs to examine. Other times its chemicals make its mind race like a hunted gazelle.

But, I repeat, it is well behaved. It follows the rules of conversational etiquette, nodding when needed, speaking when required, listening when necessary. It tries to take its turn and to stay on topic. It tries not to speak with food in its mouth, but it often forgets this in its desire to answer when spoken to. It doesn't stare if it thinks it might get caught. It is usually attentive. It leans in when empathic. It cringes when confronted with images of hunger, brutality, devastation. It withdraws when pained.

It keeps its hands to itself unless invited to do otherwise. It never forces itself upon someone else. Perhaps it has at times been annoying with its insistence, but it respects others' wishes. It is never violent. In fact, it has never hit anyone in anger, although once it tried to swing at its older brother but was so outmatched that its brother simply took a side step and it fell to the floor. It has been hit, once in its teenage years by someone who thought it was moving too close to his girlfriend and once by someone who thought, with some justification, that it had treated her unfairly. It does not like being hit, which explains why it never took to football or baseball. Golf, the sport where only the ball gets hit, has always been its preferred game.

It puts itself in places where it should be. It shows up for work. It attends the right civic activities. It appears at the funerals of friends and family. It never misses any of its daughter's concerts, theatre shows, or dance recitals. It even went to PTA meetings when it thought that might be useful. It has been a reliable chauffeur. It sits in front of the television and comes to dinner when called. It is potty trained.

It welcomes its pleasures—the deep hug of reunion, the exuberant giggle of a child, the haunting image of a painting, the presence of the earth following a downpour, the wetness as salt meets the tongue, and the comfort of rocking. It seeks its pleasures in moderation; it is not hedonist, although it has wondered if that were not a mistake. Long ago, it took its thumb out of its mouth.

Perhaps its case might best be made by remembering its attraction to a single event, frivolous maybe, but seductive as any that it knows. The event happens most often when there is a chill in the air, the wind just beginning to get its teeth. The sun, slipping in and out, gives hints of its promise but not enough to let a coat fall from the chin. The body, shoulders hunched, moves through that quickening air, longer than it would like, until it reaches its car. There, once inside, it feels the sun's work surround, wrapping itself around like a blanket. In that still air, the body knows the warmth of a cocoon, remembers the comfort of the womb. But the point is this: While it might linger for a moment, it will start the car and go where it must.

So, all in all, it is well trained, obedient, even cooperative. Yet there must be more to tell than the tale of its tethering. For surely there must be an id struggling to escape, a primal scream needing to be released, a foot eager to be taken out of its mouth. No, the id, the scream, the foot are in their proper place. No telling how long that might last, but for now that provides some comfort. Still, there must be more. Perhaps what has been left out is what matters. Perhaps the stories that still need to be told are those of longings, of dreams, of prayers.

My body longs for the dance it has done with my daughter for years, the dance we call the "Silly Waltz," the waltz from *The King and I* where Yul

Brynner with his giant steps swings Deborah Kerr around and around, the waltz we do with wild abandon but do not do enough. When we dance that dance, we stop only after we fall into each other, exhausted and laughing.

My body dreams. Once it was skipping, flying down the road. It moved so smoothly, so lightly: one foot, a hop, and then another, one foot, a hop, and then another. There was no stopping it. People were staring but it didn't care. It went on and on, never tiring, never missing a step, never losing its smile. It pushed the wind and the wind pushed it. Each step was a dolphin's leap. Each step was an eagle's dive. Each step was a peacock's fan. It never looked back. And in that dream it began floating, high, higher, higher, and it was still going, still gliding, still soaring until it was only air.

My body prays to be free from its own critical eyes, to be ready, open to whatever is before it. May it embrace others. May it be present. Once itself, may it relax. Once, just once, may it be naked and blossom.

The Body's Speech

Speaking from my heart, I begin to share. This is not always easy, for the heart is always seeking the return of its efforts. Blood for blood is what it asks. So when speaking from the heart, I speak with caution, afraid I might be passing impurities from one chamber to another, from me to you. Valves control what gets in and what gets out. But there are times when the heart races and it cannot be stopped. Responding to the situation, it puts itself at risk.

Speaking off the top of my head, words sprout like hairs. Some are tame and fall right in place. But most are wild, as if tossed about in the wind, or coarse (some would say vulgar) in their efforts to be noticed, or even inappropriate, appearing in all the wrong spots. Usually when it matters most nothing is there—no complexity of design, no separation by parts. Just the bald facts: Nothing is there when the top of the head comes off.

Speaking my mind, I say what I mean, but its meaning just seems mean. Speaking my mind, I interrupt by asking, "Do you mind?" Seldom mindful of the consequences, I speak. With my mind full, I do not care.

Speaking over my head, she went on and on. I was trying to listen, trying to go with the flow, but the more I tried, the more I felt like I was wallowing in her sea of words. I looked around, and everyone seemed to be having smooth sailing. But I was in the middle of a squall. Her wind was ripping at my sails. I couldn't see over the rising swells. I was off course. I had no idea where I was heading. I just knew that I didn't know. Wave after wave came at me. There was no place to anchor, no navigational stars. I became queasy. I tried holding on, but everything was tossing this way and that. I was drowning in waves of confusion. Finally, after an exhausting struggle, I gave up and promised myself that I would never again enter these waters without a good compass and a life preserver to keep me afloat.

Speaking under one's breath, one acknowledges power, understands that speech can make a difference, sometimes even when it isn't heard. At such times, speech rides on the underbelly of breath to dodge the grind of angry teeth. When speaking under one's breath, one realizes that one can be forced to operate within restraints. To control speech is to control the speaker. Speaking under one's breath, one negotiates the space between silence and freedom. To speak under one's breath is to speak and to keep on living. Such claims seem true for those who live their lives in subordination. I should say, perhaps under my breath, that I cannot recall ever speaking under my breath. That is the privilege, I guess, of those of us who do not have to worry about what words we breathe in and what words we breathe out.

Speaking out, I want to be heard. I elbow my way in and take the floor. I believe that I have something to say. I speak convinced of my own perspective, confident that I have a truth to tell. I am certain that others should listen. Speaking out, I can become a witness, telling of injustice. Speaking out, I can become a fool, thinking I understand injustice.

Speaking out the side of my mouth, I utter a cowardly gibe or a razor's retort. In either case, I contort, twist into a crack. I am not wise. Crooked words slip out, corkscrewing the moment. They are rusted, bent nails ricocheting into the side of another's face.

Speaking down to me, he lined up each and every word in a neat little row, spoke each and every word as slowly and carefully as could be and nodded in rhythm with each and every word as if his head were on a spring. I was so pleased. I so like having each and every thing clearly explained to me. I so like being looked at with those wide, watchful eyes. I so like having my bottom wiped.

Speaking up, I call my body forward. Ready to lead the troops, I place my body on the line. I volunteer for point. I stay alert for tripwires, snipers, carefully placed traps. I am tense, ready to take action, ready to fight my way through if need be. I look left and right. I move one step at a time. The jungle quiets as I begin, except for some recognizable noises off in the distance. I go slowly at first, but as I proceed, I gain confidence and speed. Each step is more firmly planted as I hack my way through, but I am never without caution. When I reach a clearing, I stop. I turn to my troops, wanting to know what they think, wanting to be appreciated for what I've done, wanting to relax in the company of friends.

Speaking with everyone is like sleeping around—no one really matters. It is the politician's handshake, the minister's smile, the clerk's nod ending a transaction. Speaking with someone is the moment before two lovers embrace—only the other matters. It is the smell of waiting ointments, the feel of laughter's deep rumble, the taste of another's rose wine.

The Speaking Body's Physiology

Sound is produced by making air vibrate as it is pushed through the vocal folds, pushed from the lungs to the mouth where it is shaped and launched by the tongue, that salty snake that slips around, sliding here and there in its dark cave, by the teeth that stand guard, and by the lips that press together before putting syllables out that father differing figures and that kiss words in the wonder of good-bye.

Speaking Nonverbally

Scene 1: She didn't know she was being watched, but she saw her: a woman, early thirties, confident, even though at that moment she was alone. She seemed bored, ready for something to happen. She was taking everything in without effort, without much interest. Her legs were crossed and bounced slightly, the crease of her black pants slicing the air. Her head turned slightly, back and forth, to the right and then to the left as if to show the subtle touches of her makeup. Her shoulder-length blond hair fell across the side of her face like a veil. Her lips held a slight pout.

Scene 2: She took his extended hand, and as she did, he stepped in closer, placing his other hand on top of hers. Their eyes met and seemed to sadden. They did not speak. He bent to her hand, kissed it, perhaps longer than he should, and from that bent position, turned his head slowly up to see her eyes again. She gave a small smile, hard to decipher but holding some promise. He smiled too, broader and more inviting than hers, as he straightened and pulled her even closer. Her hand went to his cheek, touched it softly, and then she placed her head on his shoulder, looking out.

Scene 3: Two bodies come together. A room without air. Wax from the burnt candle drips down. The blinds are shut. The bed, unmade. The spring flowers in the vase, dead. They are standing, flesh to flesh, connected, leg inside leg, chest to chest. Their hands, together, holding a knife. It seems as if he is whispering something in her ear but he is not. He smells her damp hair, takes her in. She feels small against his weight. Sweat slides down and tastes of salt. They do not move.

The Allure of the Alliterative Body

I have always loved, despite critics' counsel concerning its coarse and uncomplicated character, how the alliterative teases the tip of the tongue. I try tracing my attraction, try teaching it new tricks, and try not to forget its troubling deceit. I know seductive sounds need not escort sense. Even so, I write alliterations of self-indulgence and celebration, trying to avoid the trap of truth.

I worry over the speech that weakens when it does not have the breath to whisk it along, when it wobbles as it nears its end. Such speech is shallow as a grave, desperate.

I vocalize "om" over and over again until its vibration verifies the omnipresence of my body and vanishes my venomous verbosity. Then I quote my body verbatim, voicing verse after verse. I am vulnerable, vindicated, and without verdict.

I wallow in words I cannot pronounce, articulate sound I cannot apprehend.

I speak in resonance, harmonizing, ringing with reasons for reaching others. I rejoice, relish those who might reach for me. Romantic as a rose, I cover my thorns.

I sing with as much sound as I can muster Jose Feliciano's "I've Just Gotta Get a Message to You" to no one. I sing with as much sound as I can muster "Bring Him Home" from *Les Miserables* so I can pretend to snatch a day out of nothing.

I live on the tip of my tongue, ready to trade a word for a word, a toast for a toast, a titter for a titter. Sometimes I tattle, tell tales. Sometimes I testify to the triumph of connection. Sometimes I twitter with the thrill of it all. Life is an intimate interview.

I slump through sentences at a slug's pace, sucking the life from consonants and vowels along the way. I scrub adjectives and adverbs away. I skip nouns, dismiss pronouns. I erase conjunctions.

I make substitutions, breaking off endings, insisting on a linguistic style that's on my side.

I live my life in a monotone, without variety, intoning the same questions over and over, intoning the names of the dead. I live in the hope of a falling inflection.

I boast. A boisterous bohemian, I know no bounds. I breathe in broken syllables.

I speak with a nasal whine, wondering what went wrong, wondering why, when I speak, I only hear wisps of what I want to say. I speak with a nasal whine because I never know where I should begin.

I luxuriate in the liquid alliterations, leaning in to listen. They are loquacious litigations on behalf of bodily longing. Alliterations are the body's balm.

Speech Lessons for the Body

Stand up straight, speak out. Project. Let everyone hear you. Use good breath support. Speak from your diaphragm. Don't yell. Say what you want to say clearly. Articulate. Don't swallow your words. Make sure you have all the correct pronunciations. Watch your diphthongs. Rid yourself of any noticeable dialect. Avoid dropping the endings of your words. Don't speak too quickly or too slowly. Use pauses for dramatic effect, but remember, slow speech gives the impression of a slow mind. Work for a full, resonant voice, a voice that takes command. Stop whining. Eliminate that unpleasant nasal sound. Add variety. Alter your pitch, rate, and volume. Do you want to end every sentence with a rising inflection?

Don't talk behind people's back. Don't talk ugly about others. If you don't have anything nice to say, don't say anything at all. Don't interrupt. Don't walk between two people who are talking. Don't dominate the conversation. Let others have their turn to speak. Don't use offensive language. Don't be rude. Always say "thank you," "excuse me," and "please." Pay attention. Don't fall asleep when others are speaking. Nod to show you are listening. Don't stare. Speak when spoken to but don't speak with food in your mouth. Don't speak during performances. Don't speak just to hear yourself speak. Answer people's questions. Don't mumble. Think before you speak. Put your money where your mouth is. If you talk the talk, you better walk the walk. Don't ask if you don't want to know. Look at me when you talk.

Learn your "I" sounds.

The Body's Facts and Figures of Speech

FACT: According to Julia T. Wood, "Studies of people, ranging from college students to professionals, show that the average person spends 45 percent to 53 percent of waking time listening to others" (134).

FIGURE: Statistics remove the individual like a summer rain washes away chalk.

FACT: According to Teri Gamble and Michael Gamble, "On the average, we listen at only 25-percent efficiency" (38).

FIGURE: The ear is most attuned to the heart.

FACT: According to Seymour Fisher, "people have difficulty in visualizing accurately the size of certain parts of their bodies. They are especially likely to overestimate their head dimensions" (2).

FIGURE: His head held the entire alphabet; his heart a single letter.

FACT: According to Peggy Phelan, "The visible body, then, like the word, conceals rather than reveals the real of its being" (69).

FIGURE: Beneath the head is the body; beneath the body is the heart; beneath the heart is what matters.

FACT: According to Drew Leder, "The physician is a hermeneut, reading the text of the surface body for what it has to say about corporeal depths" (51).

FIGURE: The body gives its word, only to take it back again.

FACT: According to Julius Fast, "Somehow it is a great deal easier for many people to look at each other's bodies after having touched them" (81).

FIGURE: It is not the cheekbones, but that slight, falling indentation underneath; it is not the breasts, but the slow curve of their bottom line; it is not the hips, but that skin, translucent and so soft, that slides toward the center.

FACT: According to Mark L. Knapp, "Generally, Americans do not rely on their sense of smell for interpersonal cues unless perspiration odor, breath, or some other smell is unusually strong" (76).

FIGURE: Smell the naked world. Take it in like air, daily, moment to moment. Rest your head on its belly.

Speaking with the Body

Something just didn't smell right. I had been eyeing the situation and I knew that I'd have to put my foot down. I gave him an earful. I had to get it off my chest. I yelled my head off. I was so mad, I even shot him the finger. The whole situation was out of hand. I've got to hand it to him, he stood up for his own position. He said he needed more elbow room. It just turns my stomach to think what happened. There was a time when I was head over heels for him, but I wouldn't dare turn my back on him now. He could talk his arm off and I still wouldn't trust him. He is nothing but a back-stabber. What he did makes me just throw up my hands. If he ever does anything like that again, I'll be gone in a blink of an eye. In my heart of hearts, I know I'll never love him again with all my body and soul. My heart is broken. This whole thing has put an awful taste in my mouth.

The Mute Body

The mute body is hidden, covered in cotton or corduroy; it will not show itself, ashamed of its own design, of what it can and cannot do. Once, it was stripped and it felt as if its own eyes had no right to see. Its hands became sheets. It will not be skinned.

The mute body is ignored, dismissed in a glance. It knows it shouldn't show itself, shouldn't be where it doesn't belong, shouldn't try to speak. It sits in the corner, searching for a friendly face. It is never seen.

The mute body is troubling. It is addressed, anticipating an answer. It is poked, wanting some response. It is tormented, demanding that it behave. It is beaten. It continues to speak.

The mute body is forgotten. It is a dusty museum, used only for storage. It never opens its doors. Everything remains boxed.

The mute body is all hands, posing, curving, punctuating as it slides from claim to claim, clamoring in its silence.

The mute body is inept, unable to control itself, to process its own desires, to present its own perspective. It trips in open fields. It flails its indignation. It fails to figure.

The mute body is spent, troubled by its lack of composure. It tries to put itself back in place, collect itself, before its deep sigh signals the end, before sleep, before it becomes, once again, a vacuum taking in air.

The mute body is still, without breath. It never looks like itself, there, on display, waxed and set. That rigid body, resting in its coffin bed, is the reason for all the talk. Shocked by its own dismissal, it will return to dust.

On Speaking Terms with the Body

We are cautious friends whose lives are intertwined, connected so intricately that we do not know where one of us begins and the other ends. We depend upon one another. Yet we do not have much trust between us, afraid the other will become a betrayer, if not today, then tomorrow. We stand guard, watching for signs. We can be devious as we move about. We accept each other for what we are but we are always muscling for position. We have a long and troubled history, each trying to wrestle the other down, each claiming his superiority, each with his own needs. We are a tongue inside a heart.

To Speak the Body

To speak the body is to live in its centeredness. It is to articulate the heart of the matter. When all is said, it is the body that is done.

To speak the body is to know the body's moorings, to sense how the body is chained down, anchored in a sea of language. It is to anticipate the times when the body might break free.

To speak the body is to transgress, to say, as if in polite company, what shouldn't be mentioned. To move your mouth is a political act.

To speak the body is to comprehend that all speaking is a desire to have an audience, to be heard, to be held, if only for a moment. Speech knows that the body is its reason.

Works Cited

Fast, Julius. *Body Language*. New York: Pocket Books, 1971.

Fisher, Seymour. *Body Consciousness*. Englewood Cliffs, NJ: Prentice Hall, 1973.

Gamble, Teri, and Michael W. Gamble. *Public Speaking in the Age of Diversity*. Boston: Allyn and Bacon, 1994.

Knapp, Mark L. *Nonverbal Communication in Human Interaction*. New York: Holt, Rinehart and Winston, 1972.

Leder, Drew. *The Absent Body*. Chicago: University of Chicago Press, 1990.

Phelan, Peggy. *Unmarked: The Politics of Performance*. New York: Routledge, 1993.

Wood, Julia T. *Communication Mosaics*. Belmont, CA: Wadsworth, 1998.

CHAPTER 5

Mirror Mirror

I present myself before you. I am ready to see, to recognize my strange double.

You've come here asking? You've come here wondering what I can tell you? You know my only rule: You are accountable. I speak as truth's ally. That's why I so seldom see you.

When we begin to speak, we chat like old friends who, after some time apart, suddenly happen across each other. Our affection is deep. Yet I feel cautious, self-conscious.

Old friends seek each other out, enjoy each other's company, linger together. Their affection is deep. But you are mainly uneasy, afraid, aloof. You might pause for a brief moment, but then you are on your way. Your questions are quick and make for easy answers. I tell if your hair is in place, if corn is stuck between your teeth, if a pimple has come to a head. You usually ask nothing more. Now you come wanting more, claiming connections we've never had.

We are connected, like wind and chimes. Be grateful I am here. You need me as I need you. I've come clinking and clanking, catching my breath, ready to listen. I want nothing more, nothing less. I come out of necessity.

What's the necessity? Why do you come now, after all the years of letting me, to use your metaphor, hang on a rusted, bent nail?

Because of our hollow, thin notes, our broken strings and because there is so little time.

Then begin, if you must, by describing what you see. But remember, I will not be the dear lost friend or the sad chimes of your making. I will be a python, sliding out, circling, tightening around your body.

I'll try to start. I see a person with large facial features culminating in a pointed balding head. He has brown frog-eyes and black-and-gray crabgrass hair. Errant white hairs escape from his wiry eyebrows. More hair protrudes, just slightly, from his nose and ears. On the top of his left earlobe, three more hairs grow. His face is round, fat really, and his skin droops under his eyes and chin. On his left cheek are three raised bumps of discolored skin, cancerous perhaps. A thick neck, rounded shoulders, and a small chest accentuate his potbelly. Moles dot the dry skin. Below the waist—athlete's foot, trunklike legs, and an unremarkable penis.

You disgust me, not because you are such a pathetic sight, but because of your motives for saying such a thing.

What do you mean?

Come now, did you believe that those words would not be understood as a rhetorical ploy, a play for a counterclaim? Do you want me to argue that you're not being fair to yourself, that you're fine physical specimen? I won't. What you describe is accurate, even though you don't see yourself in such negative ways. You should. Besides, presenting your nude body behind a closed bathroom door is irrelevant to why you are here.

What would you have me say? You said I spoke accurately.

You can speak accurately without telling the truth. I want the truth.

You make that demand as if truth were in your possession, as if you would know it when you heard it. What truth would you have me tell?

I want the truth about why you are here, looking, searching. I want you to be accountable for your actions.

I'll say that I've tried. I've tried to be a good man, good as anyone, good as one could expect, good as a fallen priest.

So is this your confession, your act of repentance?

No, I stand before you as a witness who has seen it all, a witness who is willing but does not know how to speak in his own defense. This morning outside my window I saw a mourning dove slip on the ice as it tried to get the frozen birdseed from the feeder. I laughed as if the dove were a clown taking a pratfall for my pleasure. I laughed at the stupid bird. I am here to tell of my pratfalls, of my stupidity. I am an overstuffed pigeon.

How generous of you. And to think I thought you were setting yourself up as a sacrificial lamb, a sweet little lamb ready to offer yourself up. But no, you claim you're a fat pigeon. Lamb or pigeon, it doesn't matter. You are still just strategizing how to situate yourself as a sacred cow.

I was telling you how I feel. I know I am not beyond criticism. This is in fact an assessment of life, our life.

For whom? Surely not for me. I bet you intend to take our conversation and make it public. You'll try to write our life as example, as error, as epigraph. And you won't even notice that your story of the mourning dove is not about pratfalls but about starvation. But do not let me stop you. Proceed.

There have been lovers, children, friends—betrayed. There have been promises, dreams—forgotten. There has been emptiness. Sometimes, watching television, I'll feel as if I'm going to cry when some little display of emotion, some trite little drama, occurs—a cat is rescued from a tree, a child is given a big hug, a person is promised love. I feel the tears well up and, embarrassed, I turn away. I do not let the tears come. Sometimes, watching movies, when the lights are down, I'll let them come. I'll let them slice down my face like razors. Sometimes, laying in the dark, I will stare at nothing. Frightened, I cannot close my eyes.

Do you want sympathy or a therapist?

I want neither. I want to tell what I know. I want to say how I feel. I want . . .

The talking cure?

No, simply connection.

A little electrical charge, a little jolt, a little shock?

No. I live in the world as if covered in ice. I want a little treatment that will let me thaw.

Tell about your student, the one you truly care about, who was upset about her work and needed your support. You know, the one you froze out.

I was writing. I didn't want to be interrupted. I said a few words to her.

You never moved from your computer. Cold as an icicle, you just sat there, blowing a chilling wind full of clichés in her direction. And the irony that you were writing a poem of love even you couldn't miss.

I am entitled to some time on my own. You want more than I can give.

No, you want to get more than the little you give. That's why you are here, waiting to thaw. That's why you stare in the dark. That's why you do not recognize your own arrogance.

Arrogance? I abhor arrogance!

You can't see it in yourself? You think you'll be able to leave our little dialogue and put yourself on the page as a pleasure to consume. You are as arrogant as a religious zealot who thinks he holds all the answers.

I have no answers. That's why I'm here.

Because you want answers? Should I, like you do, hold up a metaphor for your reflection? Should I say that the light is draining from your star?

I live in the space between stars. That is where I have always resided, looking left and right, trying to see.

It is difficult to see when you have been eclipsed.

It is difficult to know what is blocking what.

And you are here to find what is on the other side of the moon.

Yes, I am a man searching for why I would often rather be alone, why there are times when I feel nothing. I am a man who looks without seeing, speaks without hearing, swallows without tasting. I am a man who could profess love without knowing what it means. I write love poems as prayers, as tragedies, as vendettas. I write to win. I move words around as if they were building blocks, as if they might make a solid foundation. But my mortar does not hold and my bricks, overbaked, crack. Words are all I have, but they never hold, never get it down, never get it right. With words, I cannot caress the stars.

Words work the world to their own advantage.

My favorite possession is a picture drawn by my six-year-old daughter with chalk on black construction paper that I keep framed above my desk. In the center of the picture is a young girl floating in a cup among hundreds of stars. Holding a fishing line over the side of the cup, she has hooked the moon. A caption at the bottom of the picture reads:

I'm the star fisher
I fish for stars in the night
I have caught the moon

Written above the young girl as a thought balloon are the words, "Oops, I caught the moon again." For my daughter, catching the moon is a delightful and innocent mistake. For me, it is proof that words make us into star-fishers who are unhappy with the moon.

You blame words as you try to move them around for your own advantage, but you are a bad poet, a cliché, a predictable rhyme. Words slither from your soul but break on your bad breath.

I breathe in and out.

Waiting until you can hook something, until something takes hold?

I remember moments, pure as communion, when body and soul were one. Once, with shovels in hand and rain tapping on our backs, my brother and I spent a day building a sand castle large enough for us both to stand in. Others came, and we put them to work building canals to the ocean. The cool water licked our feet. In the end, we left it there for the children to destroy and for the ocean to swallow. Walking away, we kept looking over our shoulders.

To remember what was made or what was lost?

We made photographs of our construction, one looking down ten stories from the balcony of our hotel room at the elaborate design and one of us standing together, arms draped across each other's shoulders, smiling, within our castle.

So you have a record of what was lost.

Yes. All we ever have is a record of comings and goings. Nothing ever holds.

Not even old photographs?

I was married once for seven years and now, at times, I cannot remember her name. I look at our wedding pictures and I do not recognize this lovely woman who is smiling at me, kissing me. I can tell you the cities where we lived, can describe our first apartment, can list the cars we drove, but she is gone. She is gone with the tears we shed, gone as are the promises we once made, gone on with her life. She is little more to me than the blur of night traffic.

Can memories be boxed and stored for when you are in need?

I had a friend I helped move. Box after box I pulled from the truck was marked "Memories." "Memories," I was told, "go in the living room." I wish it were that easy.

What is in your living room?

Music that is never played, candles that are never lit, words that are never spoken. An unopened deck of cards sits on the table.

Can you hold the cards? Shuffle? Deal?

I can't. I used to play contract bridge, but I quit the game because I was always afraid that I wouldn't make my bid, that I wouldn't be holding the cards I said I had, that I would forget the rules.

Do you prefer solitaire?

Yes.

You're lying. If that were true, you wouldn't be here trying to look in my hand, trying to see what cards I hold.

I doubt if you have any cards worth playing.

Then leave. Go ahead. It's tiresome to hear you pine away, like Narcissus, before your own reflection.

Narcissus knew that there is always more to see.

And we both know what Freud made of him.

Enough.

At last we agree.

But I have no answers.

I know. We are broken fragments, reflecting lies, trying to escape from the cold.

Yes. We are the stubborn ivy smothering our house, tangled together by years, still trying to cling on, still trying not to die from the freezing rain.

Yes.

I am your sad double.

CHAPTER 6

Remembering Vietnam

Point

My mother says I lost my sense of humor. I was unaware. I thought I had only lost two years of my life, a wife, and a son. Now I find myself coming to you to tell of loss, to heal my wounds through stories, stories that have been coming to me for over thirty years now; stories of going there, being there, and being here; stories of history and memory; stories of sorrow and disillusionment that have allowed me to keep Vietnam where I needed it—contained, safe as a storage box, taped shut but, at this moment, slowly opening. This is a story of those stories that tried to keep the lid on but couldn't. This is a story, as Arthur Frank would have it, of repair, a gesture by a witness of life interrupted. It is a story emerging from chaos, from the "narrative wreck" I became in 1969 through 1971 as a result of the Vietnam war. It ends in its desire for a place of rest and a place where work can be done. It wants a communicative ethic that ties us together, an empathic connection that readies us for action.

Preparation for War: Going There

I had nine hours to complete on my master's degree when the notice came. I was told I had to report for duty on March 17, 1969. These were the days after student deferments could buy you some time and before a lottery ball would determine your fate. And these were the days when some young boys, much braver than I, would elect to live in Canada for the rest of their lives or would opt for prison rather than to go to Vietnam. But most young boys, like myself, would do what they were told to do. It seemed to be the best choice of the unhappy options.

Accepting that I would do what I was told to do, I thought it reasonable to request a six-week extension so that I might complete my master's. Such a request required an appeal hearing before the head of my selective-service board. So for my chance to plead my case, I flew from Dallas, where I was going to school, to New Orleans, where I had dutifully registered at eighteen years of age. The meeting was scheduled for 4:30. I was ready to say how eager I was to serve my country and how I thought I would be much better prepared to kill and maim innocent people if I had my master's in hand. As I entered for my appointed time, however, I realized that my case would have to compete with a retirement party for one of the staff. I was quickly ushered into an office full of American flags and told to have a seat. The only thing on the mahogany desk in front of me was my file. Before I had time to consider what might happen if I grabbed my file and slipped out the door, a man in full military garb entered. I stood up, prepared to shake his hand. He went straight to his desk without acknowledging my presence. He opened my file and closed it quickly. "I see you've already received your draft notice. I'm sorry I can't do anything for you," he said, tucking my file under his arm and leaving the room. It took me several minutes to realize that our meeting was over and that I would not have a chance to speak. I was stunned. On my way out, I saw him lifting a piece of cake to his mouth.

So on March 17, 1969, I kissed my wife good-bye and reported for duty. The induction center processed boys into either the army or the marines. I would like to say that I was disruptive, that I just doodled on the written tests I was required to take, or that I traded urine samples with several other guys, but the truth is, I was too scared to do anything but follow instructions. As I moved from station to station, I kept hearing rumors that most of the guys being processed would be sent to the marines, a prospect that few of us welcomed. The marines, we believed, was a direct ticket to the boonies in Vietnam. At the end of the day, I found myself sitting in a large room with about one hundred other inductees waiting to hear what would become of us. A sergeant entered and moved to the center of the room. "Everyone to my right," he said, "you are now a marine. Everyone to my left, you are now in the army." The room split down the middle with sighs and moans. Being among those who were sighing, I was sent to Fort Polk, Louisiana for the army's basic training.

Basic training, as legend has it, turns silly boys into real men, makes innocent kids into good soldiers. In the name of making good soldiers, we were
trained with the latest of techniques. In the name of making good soldiers, we
were ordered to crawl through a muddy field before we lined up for dinner.
After we got our chow, we were told we were such dirty little pigs that we had
to lick our plates clean. In the name of making good soldiers, a corporal who
caught me chewing gum when I didn't have permission made me stick the gum
in my pubic hair and display it every hour that day for the edification of the
platoon. That night I had to slowly shave my hair to get it out. The next day,
I was ordered to display my gum and, being unable to do so, I was told I was
such pervert for having a shaved pubic area that I would have to do double
what everyone else was required to do that day. In the name of making good
soldiers, our drill sergeant would come into the barracks well after lights out
and yell, "Where are all the cockroaches?" Now we had been told that whenever the drill sergeant asked, "Where are all the cockroaches?" we were supposed to lay on our backs and wiggle our arms and legs up the air. Once we
were in that position, the drill sergeant could complete the formula: "I hate
cockroaches," and his boot would land on our stomachs. After he had squished
enough cockroaches, we could return to bed. In the name of making good soldiers, we could either march to church services on Sunday morning singing
rhythmic chants about the joys of killing Vietnamese (e.g., "Family of gooks
sitting by a stream / Watch them burn and hear them scream") or spend the
day cleaning the latrine with a toothbrush. Most of us elected the cool shadows of the chapel over the cool tiles of the latrine. In the name of making good
soldiers, we were taught the difference between our weapon (read M-16) and
our gun (read penis): "Your weapon is for killing; your gun is for fun." And we
were taught that it is great fun to fire your weapon at cardboard caricatures of
Vietnamese men, women, and children on the firing range.

And good soldiers we became. We learned it is always easier to just do what
you were told, to just avoid calling any attention to yourself, and to just accept,
as their military bible puts it, "Thou shall not murder," the theological dis-
tinction between "murder" and "kill" being that killing certain people is
acceptable if sanctioned by the government, but murder can still get you court-
martialed and killed.

And having been trained in the basics, I stood waiting to hear what would
become of me next. Infantry or, to use the term of the day, grunt, was the
MOS (the army's acronym for Military Occupational Specialty) most wanted
to duck. Such an assignment was a quick jet to the rice paddies. So when I
heard my name under the MOS of medic, I was relieved until I remembered
that medics were just grunts without the infantry training. But off I went to
Fort Sam Houston in San Antonio.

There I watched army training films. Few had compelling plots or engaging characters, but I learned how to properly put on a Band-Aid, how to properly tie a sling, and how to properly take someone's temperature. I also learned that I didn't want any of us working on anyone who might be hurt. Quite simply, at the end of our training, we were incompetent. "Stop the bleeding" was the most useful phrase we had drilled into us. We just weren't sure how to stop the bleeding, the bleeding of wounded soldiers or our own. We knew it had something to do with pressure, like the pressure a cow must feel as it is held in place before slaughter.

There, if I had been a good soldier, I was able to spend weekends with my wife. There, without thinking, we conceived my son and the stakes seemed even higher. Pressed together, we lay side by side, listened for news that might signal an end to the war, and wondered how the future might pull us apart. Living in anxious anticipation was no way to live. I carried the weight of the seemingly inevitable like a sack of rotting potatoes. I could never put it down, never get it balanced on my shoulders, never get rid of the stench. And I could not talk about it. There was no story to tell or feelings to share. The story was obvious and the feelings were evident and, my wife and I thought, best hidden. Going to Vietnam was the proverbial elephant in the living room as we moved through our lives, as our son grew toward his birth.

My orders came, which gave us a short reprieve. I was to report for duty at Fort Leavenworth, Kansas. I was assigned to the intensive care and prison ward. My first day on the job, I met Rufus Hayden.

Coma on the Intensive Care Ward

A clothespin nurse handled the introductions:
"He has been here for two months; could last forever.
When you work the early shift, you'll bathe and shave him."

I started with your white whiskered face, slowly
Pulled the razor through lines of worn skin.
I washed your neck, limp arms and legs,

Wiped carefully around bed sores, sunken raw skin.
I checked wires, pulse, machines, blood pressure,
Emptied your urine bag in preparation for doctor and wife.

We learned to speak without a sound, in EKG rhythm
And each day my hands moved more easily into yours.
Machines grew on you like moles, so I cleaned them.

Your wife held your coma in her posture
As we sat in silence on stiff chairs,
Watched air move in and out your toothless mouth.

When fever struck, you sucked precious air,
Sucked holes in your room, sucked sound in your throat,
Sucked till your fever broke and machines hummed.

Daily she came, worn like a heavily used rug,
Filled your cracked flower vase, oiled your dry feet,
And each day left me with a new epitaph:

"He had one of the best stamp collections you ever saw."
"His toes turned up every single time he laughed."
"He stole wine from the Germans during the war."

When the next fever came, doctors covered you like blinds.
"Temperature 106. Pulse faint. Blood pressure weak."
"Not much we can do now. I guess we'll let him go."

Fever fried your flesh and roasted your chalk bones.
Parched machines coughed blood and then stopped.
You softly sank from us deeper and deeper into bed.

He died on the day I received my orders for Vietnam. He died one month before I was scheduled to go and one month before my wife was scheduled to give birth. He died the day before I requested an extension to be present for my son's birth and was denied. He died two weeks before my son, perhaps recognizing the urgency, was born. He died one month before I kissed my son and wife good-bye and left for Vietnam.

Rearguard Report 1

Remembering begins in the body, in vague feelings, in the sensuous before it claims its story. Memory is made from traces, fragments, and images, from what cannot be let go, from what insists on a psychic place. It is a record of what is deemed worthy of collection and recollection. And so, on memory's insistence, I tell my tales of going there. I tell them with a sense of injustice, of cynicism, and, despite what my mother might think, I think with a sense of dark humor. I tell them whenever they might be needed, whenever the conversation might turn in their direction, whenever the "what was it like?" question might encourage their appearance. Each telling stands as a basis for future reminiscences, and with time, they settle into place. Set, they become available for use without pain, healed and unremarkable scars. They are part of my personal archives, easily accessed, always ready to make me into them.

The Battle: Being There

I stood in formation alongside an airfield near Saigon and I waited for my orders. On the full and silent flight over, we didn't know where we would be placed, didn't know what we would be asked to do, didn't know anything but rumors. We just knew we would be assigned to the space someone else had left, either by rotating out or by black bag. A sergeant called my name and Chu Lai and then, laughing, added, "Rocket City." That night when the sirens sounded and the rockets rained down, I scrambled to a bunker. In my haste, I cut my leg on the rusted barbed wire just outside the bunker. Blood rolled down my shaking body. My eyes were cartoon wide. After a short time, I noticed that several men were there. We nodded to each other but did not speak. One of them unlocked a half-buried chest and pulled out a candle, a bottle of Jack Daniels, and playing cards. They drank and gambled throughout the night as the rockets continued to fall. I tried to take some comfort in their game, but I had never felt so afraid, so alone.

I was assigned to a medical evac company overlooking an inlet on the China Sea. The base was considered safe. The hooch I shared with five other guys was big enough for each of us to have a bed, a foot locker, and a steel 3x3x6 cabinet and an old round table for all of us to share. Around that table, we smoked dope and listened to the Beatles, Janis Joplin, and Jimi Hendrix on our reel-to-reel Sony tape deck. The walls were covered with posters—my favorite pictured a peace sign and the simple words underneath: "Stop the War." The rain would drop down on the tin roof like tiny rockets. The sun would make the hooch the target of its flames. Around the bay at night, we could see the flares shot into the air by those on guard. U.S. jets would provide their own fireworks display. During the day, we would go for a swim.

The tops of the hills were bald as a bosom, bombed free of all life except for green uniforms scurrying for survival whenever an attack would come. And they would come, mostly after dark, filling the nights with sounds of fear and pain, with sounds of death. Bodies were torn, gutted by metal. Wounds of burnt flesh and tumbling bullets would make their way into the ward. In daylight, the perimeter would be searched. The surrounding foliage would be ripped, broken, soiled with blood. The bodies would be counted. The tracks of a one-legged man, now gone, would count toward the number of wounded. Arms and legs would be left as fertilizer.

Charlie Burdick, who with genuine affection we called Bird Dick, was my best friend. He was there when I arrived and taught me what I needed to know. He demonstrated how to take blood samples fast enough that you could leave on time after your twelve-hour shift and not so fast that your patients thought you were rushing. He told me who to avoid and who to befriend. He taught me what to do when the wounded and dead came in. He showed me how to survive. Bird Dick had a master's degree in psychology and decided upon graduation that he would enlist rather than wait to be drafted. That way, he figured, he could request his MOS, even though that meant committing for four years instead of being drafted for two. He picked what the army calls "mental hygiene," a label that suggests that thinking about cleanliness is the key to good health. His recruiter failed to tell him that training in mental hygiene required training first as a medic and that once he was trained as a medic, he could be assigned to that job. So there he was, in Vietnam, with me, being my friend. Despite our deep friendship, we decided that after we left Vietnam we would never see each other again.

A second lieutenant led his men without an injury for seven heroic months in the Vietnam jungle away from the VC. Then he was court-martialed.

Mama-san, a toothless sixty-year-old, came once a week to do our laundry. As she cleaned our dirt, she pretended that she didn't understand the GI's vulgar invitations. Our barber cut our hair by day and fought with the VC by night. Young girls danced in the clubs, showing what the soldiers wanted to see. Papa-san beat the latrine tubs to frighten away the rats before he pulled them into the field to burn our shit. On good days, there were no hidden shaving-cream cans in the tubs ready to explode. Villagers spit as the grunts walked by. Children were not to be trusted.

A calendar hung over my bed marking the days until I could return home. X's told of days spent; numbers, counting backward, told of days to go. Each day the ritual of marking through another calendar square was performed. After six months, a soldier could request R and R, a week of rest and relaxation away from Vietnam. Most of the single men went to Thailand; most of the married men flew to Hawaii to meet their wives. Going back home was not an option. I flew to Hawaii, anticipating a blissful week with my wife. It never occurred to either of us that we would have changed. It seemed particularly odd to me that she would find the movie *Mash* funny.

He came in by chopper, shot just below the ribs. I was undressing his field bandage to see what he faced when I noticed it. Ears. Ears hooked on his belt. The ears hooked on his belt had turned black.

The policy was clear. If a soldier was not circumcised, he could request the operation. The operation consisted of making two incisions around the penis about an inch apart, peeling away the extra, unwanted skin, and suturing the remaining top skin to the bottom so that the head of the penis would be uncovered. The procedure was painful. Yet soldier after soldier lined up for the operation, not because they believed it was a matter of hygiene as the army policy suggested or because they wanted a different bodily aesthetic, but because it required about three weeks' recovery time in a warm bed.

The men would come in from the field, stamped with dirt, savage, wild eyed, unable to sit still. They could not be washed clean. Their shocked faces could not make a smile. They could not be contained. If the company commander thought I wasn't doing my job, I would become one of them.

I was awarded the Purple Heart for injuries sustained in battle. The battle was intense, a basketball game on an open court in the late-day heat, two sides, evenly matched, playing for a case of beer. Before the game, I had had several moles removed by a buddy, and being too stoned to feel much of anything, I ripped the stitches out. "Wounded in conflict," the company commander who was playing center for my team said. I also received the Bronze Star for outstanding service, an award I was given, not as a joke, but because of the job I had done. I am embarrassed to say this, but I felt proud. The final checkpoint as soldiers left Vietnam was a small room for picking up the awards they had earned. When my turn came, I saw a corporal sitting behind several tables filled with medals and campaign ribbons reading the *Stars and Stripes*. Without looking up, he told me to take whatever I wanted.

When a prostitute was brought on base, word spread quickly. With their twenties in hand, the men lined up outside a hooch waiting their ten-minute turn. Her eyes just stared at the ceiling.

We've got a collapsing lung here. We've got a fractured femur here. We've got a punctured intestine here. We've got a DOA here.

Rearguard Report 2

"Sometimes I feel history slipping from my body / like a guilty bone," poet Lucia Perillo writes. I wonder if the fragments I allow myself to remember hold the story I need to tell. I can offer little more than moments, glimpses into another time and place that yearn for a beginning, middle, and end; that seek a coherent plot; and that want a moral as sweet and sure as Aesop's. I give what I have, knowing I am an inadequate witness and knowing, too, that what is missing in what I have to give may be where my story lives. I cannot tell what it means to live with these memories, to keep them buried, to try to hold them still. I cannot tell how remembering or forgetting might make or heal me. I cannot tell if what I tell is enough.

Memory is volatile. Sometimes, memory's tales just won't do the work they are asked to do. They just won't settle, won't arrange themselves so that they might be left alone. They are like scabs itching to be picked. They are wounds always ready to bleed again.

A Soldier's Return: Being Here

I was in Vietnam on a Friday. On Saturday, I traveled home. On Sunday, my wife, holding my son in her arms, said she wanted a divorce. On Monday, I was sitting in a Performance of Poetry class. Performing poetry seemed quite silly. I managed to continue the silliness long enough, however, to get my master's degree.

My degree culminated in a production that stood as my first public protest against the war. Informed by the writings of Marshall McLuhan, this multimedia show worked by juxtaposing images—slides of flower arrangements with slides of atrocities from Vietnam, clips from war movies with clips from the evening news about Vietnam, slides of people walking the avenues of Disney World with slides of soldiers moving through the jungles of Vietnam, the national anthem with protest songs, and much more. During this media barrage, performers read poetry protesting the war. In retrospect, I know the show was too heavy-handed, too didactic, too sermonizing, but even now, I don't think of it as silly. And after securing my first teaching position, it didn't seem silly when I joined the Veterans Against the War.

We had covered the campus with fliers announcing the rally against the war—12:00 on the Quad. When the announced day arrived, we were ready, had planned our speeches about the injustices of the war, and had even invested in a small bullhorn powerful enough to reach a small crowd. Seven of us, partially dressed in clothing left over from our Vietnam days, began our rant against the war, and after about fifteen minutes had managed to gather a crowd of about five. Now the university surely did not want to infringe on anyone's freedom of speech but using a bullhorn was against university policy. To make sure that university policy was followed, five police cars, sirens wailing, descended from all directions. Our crowd of five grew. And when a police officer threw one of the speakers to ground and cuffed him so he wouldn't use that bullhorn again, the crowd grew even bigger. And when the crowd began to chant their protest, the police officers called for backup, and when the backup arrived, sirens wailing, the crowd grew even more. And when a police officer, who was feeling that the crowd was getting bigger and louder than he liked, thought he had better club a few of the more vocal members of the crowd just to show who was in control, the crowd grew some more. And when a police officer decided the solution to the problem was to fire tear gas into crowd, the crowd was larger than we had ever imagined might show up for the rally. And by the time the crowd demanded that Senator Mark Hatfield, one of the first senators to speak out against the war, address them instead of giving his scheduled speech to the College of Agriculture on an upcoming bill on farm subsidies, the only place where everyone would fit was on the Quad. Sensing the explosive mood of the crowd, Senator Hatfield spoke softly into the bullhorn the police provided: "Let us first have a moment of silence for the students who lost their lives at Kent State." And the crowd fell silent. The next day the paper claimed that thousands of students participated in a violent protest against the war. Led by outside agitators, the paper went on, the students caused considerable damage to campus property. Thirty-eight students were arrested. I never gave my speech that day.

Nor did I give any antiwar speeches after that day. I found myself trying to move on with my life. After some time, I puzzled over why others could not get on with their lives. About five years later, I found myself driving through Hayti, Missouri, the place Bird Dick was from. I had stopped for gas on my way to visit my parents and decided I would see if I could find his number. I sat in the phone booth afraid to call, afraid to break our agreement. I sat there remembering our time together. Then it hit me: He was, except for members of my family, the first man I loved. My shaking finger ran down the B's. Burdick, Charles was not there. There were no Burdicks. Sad and relieved, I cried for what brought us together and what keeps us apart.

The next time I found myself in tears over the war was several years later in front of the Vietnam War Memorial. Row after row of names. Row after row in stark simplicity. Row after row, with names of soldiers I might have prepared for their black-bag flight home. I asked a volunteer who would help you locate any names you wanted to find to tell me where I might find Charlie Burdick.

"How do you spell that?" he said.

I gave the spelling.

"Are you sure?"

"Yes, I'm sure."

"We don't have anyone by that name listed."

"Good," I answered, breathing more easily. "Would you check another name for me? Kippy Moppert, I mean Gene. Gene Moppert." I knew my old childhood friend, Kippy, was there. Given the needed numbers, I went right to him. I went right to him, fell on my knees, and cried. A man about my age I had never seen before knelt beside me. He put his arm around me and said, "I know. I know. I was there."

And even after all this time, I find that I am still there. I don't know why, but I teasingly ask my family every Veterans Day where is my Veterans Day present. They have never given me one. I don't know why, but I still have the hat I was issued in Vietnam. I wear it sometimes when I play golf. I don't know why, but I am drawn to war films; I have a sense that I must see them. Always I leave feeling depressed. I don't know why, but every time I see that a documentary on Vietnam is being shown, I have to watch. I cheer for both sides. I don't know why I never have been able to find the humor in *Mash*, the movie or the television show. I don't know why every year when I go to a fireworks display on the Fourth of July, I go to Vietnam. And I don't know why I had to write this poem just last summer.

Answers

Before the afternoon summer sun
decided to end its work, a man
sped past on a bike, Asian,
dressed all in black, perhaps
Vietnamese, and in that second
waves of heat, of people coming

from small thatched roof houses,
coming from all directions,
some walking with their burdens,
some pedaling across dirt roads,
some coming over hills
I had no desire to defend.
We were all doing our daily tasks.
Mine were medic's hands
trying to undo what had been
done, trying not to see what
I had to work on, flesh, torn,
burnt, beside bones that were
broken, twisted, reaching
toward the ignited sky.

On the side of the road
a bike was overturned,
its pedals bent and still,
the spokes of the front wheel
blown out, made into spikes,
from the dropped bomb
landing on its target.
In the dry ditch below
a small group, looking down,
questioning her, jabbing
with the ends of their rifles
at her shrapnel wounds
that I was there to mend.
"Ask her, where are the VC.
Where?" the major yelled
first to the translator
and then to her. "Where?"
My hands' poor work
could not stop
her body's preference for
death over answers.

He was still in black
when I saw him next.
He walked into my rhetoric

class at the end of the hour,
walked dead in front
of me while I was lecturing.
I just stood there, looking,
my hands white with chalk.
"I forgot my work."
Reaching under a desk,
he pulled out a worn tablet.
"In here," he said,
"are the notes for the test."

Summary Report

In the end, I do not know if the stories I tell about going there, being there, and living in its aftermath are tales of recovery or tales of symptoms. I do not know if the wound continues to live in the scar. I do not know what is my duty to remember and my duty to forget. I do know that in the telling I become my stories, become a person who reaches for stories out of need, who, as Polkinghorne suggests, "revises, selects, and orders past details in such a way as to create a self-narrative that is coherent and satisfying and that will serve as a justification for one's present condition and situation" (106). I do not always succeed.

And I do not succeed or fail alone. Remembering is a collective act, something we do together. It is created in discourse, in our interaction, in this moment (Middleton and Edwards; Connerton). Memory is not what emerges from an individual mind but what emerges from social life. So together we share the burden of what is to be told. As Broda-Bahm writes, "History is a tale we tell in order to contextualize our current moment" (118). What we decide to remember says who we are now. It is our ongoing testimony, our work as witnesses. What we commemorate each day by the telling of our tales is our necessary history and our moral mandate. In the chew of memory, we only have our contested pasts and plausible accounts, continually told and retold in good faith, to lead us to the future.

Works Cited

Broda-Bahm, Chris. [Untitled]. *The Future of Performance Studies: Visions and Revisions*. Ed. Sheron J. Dailey, 118–20. Annandale, VA: National Communication Association, 1998.

Connerton, Paul. *How Societies Remember*. Cambridge: Cambridge University Press, 1989.

Frank, Arthur. W. *The Wounded Storyteller: Body, Illness, and Ethics*. Chicago: University of Chicago Press, 1995.

Middleton, David, and Derek Edwards, eds. *Collective Remembering*. London: Sage, 1990.

Perillo, Lucia Maria. "The Northside at Seven." *Dangerous Life*. Boston: Northeastern University Press, 1989.

Polkinghorne, Donald E. *Narrative Knowing and the Human Sciences*. Albany, NY: State University of New York Press, 1988.

CHAPTER 7

For Father and Son:
An Ethnodrama with
No Catharsis

Genre

It's a mystery. What happened? How did we get here? What will happen next? Is there some character who will come on stage and explain it all? What details are needed to make everything clear? What loose ends need to be tied up? Whom should we fear? Whom should we not trust? Who will surprise us in the end? Is it explainable? Is there an author?

It's a futurist one-act. The curtain opens. A phone sits on a table. A man looks at the phone. It does not ring. Curtain.

It's a farce, performed by characters cast in different plays. The scenes repeat themselves. No character enters when another is on stage, no character talks with another, no character speaks the truth. All characters are ridiculous.

It's a melodrama in which I am the villain twirling my son's mustache.

It's a tragedy that is based on a simple tragic flaw. There is no Oedipal drive, no Promethean heroism, no Narcissian vanity. It is a simple case of avoidance. Out of mind, there is no problem. Out of mind, there is no need for contact. Out of mind, there are no promises.

It's a comedy of manners where I, the fumbler, never quite know what is right.

It's an absurdist drama. The curtain opens. Two phones sit on a table. A man looks at the phones. A phone rings. He picks up the receiver of the one not ringing. "Hello. Hello?" he calls out. He hangs up and cries out, "There must be more phones." He leaves the stage and returns with another phone. The pattern repeats itself until the stage is filled with phones. He never selects the phone that rings. His final words are, "Hello. I said, 'hello.' Can't you hear me? Is anyone there? Hello? Hello?" Curtain.

It's a comedy of errors, but no one is laughing.

Plot

It tells how a father could let his son become involved with the wrong crowd, become involved with drugs, become someone else.

It tells how a son never listened to anyone, except those he shouldn't.

It tells how a father's guilt can lead in the opposite direction to his desire.

It tells how the space between the reader and writer is the page and how the space between father and son is the heart.

It tells how families are formed and forgotten.

It tells how inaction becomes an action.

It tells how a son resents his father for never being there, for never being what a father should be, for rejecting him and how he still seeks his father's approval.

It tells how a father cannot bring himself to give his son the approval he desires.

It tells how heredity can leave no mark, no claims, no love.

It tells how stepfathers can triumph over fathers, how allegiance can trump blood, how ties can untwist.

It tells how time figures and fixes fate.

It tells how sadness becomes set, etched in memory, settled as a scar.

It tells how silence is a strategy, an ongoing conversation between two listeners.

Characters

Father: middle-aged man who wants to say, "Son, come here."

Son: mid-twenties man who wants to say, "Father, why?"

Wives, stepfathers, daughters, grandparents, friends: various ages, who constantly say, "I don't know what to say."

Thought

You want, as a father, to be the father that your father was. You want to be present. You want to say what is possible and pertinent. You want to show what can be. You want to believe in your father's words. You want them to hold steady.

You want, as a son, your father to be the father you never had. You understand absence. You cannot speak. You do not know what you represent. You listen for your father's words, but you hear no sounds. Nothing is secure. You have nothing to repeat.

Scenes

Scene 1: Divorced Parents Discuss Their Child

MOTHER: I won't have it. I won't. I'll not have him living in my house any longer.

FATHER: I can understand that. You have every right to feel that way. I wouldn't want him and his friends in my house doing drugs either.

MOTHER: Well, what are you going to do?

FATHER: I don't know what I can do. I'll talk to him if you like.

MOTHER: Don't you think I've tried that?

FATHER: I'm sure you have.

MOTHER: I can't live like this any longer.

FATHER: Tell him to move.

MOTHER: I've told him I want him to, but he won't get out. He says he doesn't have enough money to get a decent place.

FATHER: If we give him any money, he'll just blow it on drugs.

MOTHER: I was thinking that if we got him an apartment and if we paid the rent, then he couldn't blow it on drugs. And he would be away from here. I have to get him out of my house.

FATHER: Should we be paying his rent? Isn't it time he took on some responsibility?

MOTHER: All I know is that I want him out of my house.

Scene 2: A Conversation between Father and Son

FATHER: I'm not going to give you $10,000 for another car. I'm sorry. That's just too much.

SON: Well, I guess I'll have to ask my grandmother again. I just don't think I should always be asking her to bail me out.

FATHER: Right. I don't think you should either.

SON: Well, I gotta have a car.

FATHER: Yeah, but you do not need a $10,000 T-Bird.

SON: You just want me to buy a piece of shit.

FATHER: No. I want you to buy something reasonable, something that will be reliable, something that will get you to work every day.

SON: That T-Bird is a reliable car. It's in great shape.

FATHER: The last thing you need is another car that calls attention to itself.

SON: That car is like a family car.

FATHER: Yeah, right.

SON: How much are you willing to put in?

FATHER: Depends on what car you're talking about.

SON: So you won't even pitch in a few thousand dollars? I mean, if you put a few thousand, then I think grandma would go the rest.

FATHER: You're missing the point.

SON: No, you are. I've gotta have a car.

Scene 3: A Husband and Wife Plan for His Arrival

WIFE: I wish he wasn't coming.

HUSBAND: I can't tell my son he can't come to the house on Christmas.

WIFE: I know, but he'll just ruin the day. I hate how he always gets to you.

HUSBAND: Maybe he won't stay long.

WIFE: Is he expecting to have Christmas dinner with us?

HUSBAND: I don't know. I didn't say anything to him about it.

WIFE: When is he coming?

HUSBAND: I told him to come around 2:00.

WIFE: Is he planning to spend the night?

HUSBAND: I don't know. We didn't discuss it.

WIFE: I would just like to know what to prepare for.

Scene 4: Another Conversation between Father and Son

FATHER: How long have you been working as a roofer now?

SON: Eight years.

FATHER: Wow. I didn't realize it was for so long. Are you getting any benefits?

SON: No.

FATHER: No? What would happen if you fell?

SON: I know how to move up there. You just go, go, go. You don't think about it.

FATHER: Anyone could fall.

SON: I've fallen a couple of times. Never really got hurt though.

FATHER: You're lucky.

SON: I guess, but I can't imagine myself doing this work when I'm thirty-five. My legs are already giving out. When I'm carrying a load of shingles up a ladder, my legs just shake.

FATHER: That should tell you something.

SON: I can't do anything else and make enough money. I'm not a brain surgeon.

FATHER: You were a smart kid.

SON: That was long ago.

FATHER: Before you fucked yourself up on drugs.

SON: Don't start.

FATHER: I'm not. I'm just saying that you were smart.

SON: I'm not fucking with that shit anymore.

FATHER: Good.

SON: I can't. If I just go near it, I'm fucked.

FATHER: Well, stay away. (*Silence.*) So, you gave Jenny a ring?

SON: Yeah.

FATHER: And what does that mean to you?

SON: I don't know.

FATHER: Are you planning to get married?

SON: Not now. We can't afford a wedding.

FATHER: It only takes a few bucks to go to the justice of the peace.

SON: Yeah, I guess. But things are going along fine now. We don't want to mess anything up.

FATHER: Is Jenny still stripping?

SON: Yeah.

FATHER: Are you okay with that?

SON: I don't get jealous, if that's what you mean. Sometimes I go watch her. I'll say to some guy sitting next to me at the bar, "See that girl. I'm going home with her tonight." He'll say, "No way," and before you know it, I've made a twenty.

FATHER: Does Jenny get any benefits?

SON: No.

FATHER: What would you do if either of you got sick? Or if Jessica got sick?

SON: We survive. We get along. Just last week we went up to Chicago to hear Nine Inch Nails. We took off from work around 2:00 and hauled ass. They were awesome. We didn't get back home until around 5:30 the next morning.

FATHER: Sounds like fun. Do you have your license again?

SON: It cost me a fortune. I had to pay this lawyer a ton of money.

FATHER: For what?

SON: I kept getting pulled over while I was under suspension. I had to get to work.

FATHER: How many tickets did you get?

SON: A whole shitload.

FATHER: What is your insurance costing you now?

SON: Nothing.

FATHER: What do you mean?

SON: I don't have any insurance. I couldn't afford it. I got this guy I know to fix the records so that it showed that I had insurance so I could get my license. I had to get my license back.

FATHER: You could take public transportation or you could let Jenny drive.

SON: Jenny doesn't have her license. She never bothered to get one in Missouri after her Illinois one expired.

FATHER: So neither of you has a valid license?

SON: I have a valid license, just no insurance, and Jenny has insurance but no valid license.

FATHER: I see. That sounds like a problem to me.

SON: Well, we do what we gotta do.

FATHER: There are other options.

SON: Only for people like you, man. I don't have options. I do what I gotta do.

FATHER: Well, you "gotta do" some things for Jessica. You have some responsibility for her, even if she is Jenny's child.

SON: I'm responsible. That child listens. She knows that she better not give us any shit.

FATHER: She's a sweet kid.

SON: Yeah, but she's fucking up in school.

FATHER: What's the problem?

SON: It just takes her forever to learn anything. She's got this friend that she plays with—you tell her something and she's got it like that. (*Snaps his fingers.*) Jessica, you tell over and over, and she still doesn't get it.

FATHER: Maybe she has some kind of learning disability. Has she been tested at school?

SON: She's had some tests, but they didn't find anything.

FATHER: You'll just have to work with her. That's all you can do with your kid.

SON: Did you work with me?

FATHER: The best I knew how.

SON: Well, you fucked up, didn't you?

Scene 5: A Monologue: A Father Speaks about His Other Child

"Doug called. He wants you to call him back," my thirteen-year-old daughter reports on her half-brother. Her words break his silence of nine months, nine months without contact, without any connection with my son. "Are you going to call him back?" she asks. "Yes," I answer, but I delay doing so. My mind races to the impact of his presence on my wife, who doesn't want him in the house; on my daughter, who wants some relationship with this man; and on me, who believes in the obligation of blood, of family, of father to son but who, like his wife, doesn't want him in the house.

"Call him back," she orders and I, still delaying, say with impatience, "I will." A day passes, and then another. "Have you called Doug yet?" she wants to know, wondering how a parent could turn on a child.

Diction

Shall I claim the word "father," claim it as if I earned the right to stake such a claim? Who should I say I am? Who should I say he is? Dare I use the word "son"? He was my "dependent" who learned not to depend on me. We live a legacy of wasted words, inherit our empty intentions, and procreate the unspoken. I, who did not take on the name of father, bred a child who did not take on the name of son.

Where are the words? How can I arrange them in the right order? How can I place them in the right rhythm? How can I put them in harmony? Why won't they settle into easy iambs? Where is the rhyme and reason of it all? My words are nothing more than crusted platitudes, predictable as poison, pounding the blood from our hearts. There is nothing here but what is left unsaid.

Spectacle

Drop the fliers. Roll in the set. Start the music. Turn the lights up full. Put us on the revolving stage. Spin it faster and faster. Make it so we can hardly stand. It is a sight to see. Pull the curtain as we become a spectacle.

Waiting for Catharsis

This is a play, co-authored, that I cannot forget. I remember him at two. The night the marriage ended, I stood at the door and saw his soft smile, knowing he did not understand and knowing he never would.

I remember him at five. He called himself Dougie the Cowboy and thumped through the house on his stick horse. When I phoned, he would cry. "Be a big cowboy, stop crying. Daddy will see you soon."

"When is soon?" he asks.

"Maybe a few weeks, buddy."

"That's not soon. Come tonight."

"I can't, but it won't be long before I get to see my boy. Let me talk to your mother." Bang bang. You're dead.

"He waits by the phone every week," she says.

"When can I see him?"

"Soon," she replies.

I remember him at thirteen. Dirty from a day at school, he comes to visit. We speak rehearsed lines like actors tired from a long run. He knows he lives in a world beyond my shelves of books. "Well," I say, "how's it feel to be a teenager?" A shrug and I want to shout: Don't you realize that your years define me as much as you, that distance kept you from being my son, that time is running out, that I am not your father? Instead, we talk of weekend plans and I, like a camp counselor with a whistle around my neck, chatter on about our scheduled hours: movies, cake, and this and that until each minute is arranged to blur all contact. When our allotted time ends, we leave each other relieved, safe, ready to return to our world, having fulfilled our responsibility and feeling the lie we decided to keep.

I remember him at eighteen, graduation night. Sitting next to his mother, I watch him cross the stage. "It wasn't easy," she says under her breath. I know she is right. And as he drives away for his night of celebration, he waves goodbye to us and I think, "It's never going to be this easy again."

I remember him now, his tough, hard body beginning to crack from the years of roofing and from the years of postponed intentions. He wears his clothes as if they were oddly creased. Denying his curls, he combs his hair back, slick, as if he understood style. He walks, head turning from side to side, as if he were being watched. When he counts his money, he does so with either too much flourish or too much privacy. He fell from the middle class with a thud. He fell as I watched from my suburban home. Now he falls on my couch, large, laden, lost. I offer him a Coke.

This is a play to remember. But there is no catharsis, no purging of emotions, emotions that sit inside us like jagged rocks. There is no release, no act of purification. This play ends in silence. There is no applause, no final bow. The curtain cannot close.

CHAPTER 8

The Poet's Self: Making Someone

> The purpose of poetry is to remind us
> how difficult it is to remain just one person.
>
> —CZESLAW MILOSZ, "Ars Poetica?"

I move myself around the page, dotting my i's. I am circling my o's, looping my y's, and cupping my u's. I wait until the words come to rest and their sounds settle. I seek the lines that contain and connect, that run on, that are jammed against one another and then come to a dead stop. I want shapes in perfect symmetry and shapes that snuggle against the left margin and that hang over the right's edge. I live in the breath of my making. I long to examine myself on the page, to inspect this human specimen, to classify him and be done with him. I am in search of form.

My search for form is an autobiographical quest that uses the data of everyday life, real and imagined, to articulate a self, to find a self's center. It lets me become a traveler who is always asking how I might make sense of what is before me and how I might fit in. The search for form requires, more than anything else, the maneuvering of self, sometimes putting the self forward, sometimes holding the self back; sometimes confessing, sometimes testifying; sometimes sticking to the facts, sometimes using fiction to tell the truth. It is the making and unmaking of masks. My task, then, is always a rhetorical one. It requires a persuasive strategy deployed on my own and the reader's behalf that locates the self appropriate to the moment. As I work my way, the self is always there, demanding its negotiation.

Dotting My "I's"

To place a mark above the "i" is a gesture toward exactness, an exercise in attending to detail, to alignment. It demands discipline, thought, and the faith that such things matter. It is a chef's final spice, a printer's final proof, an artist's final touch. Sometimes it comes as a rush to completion; sometimes it comes as a crawl to closure. It is the fool's dream that there will be no mistakes, that everything will be in its right place, that there will be precision, pinpointed, complete.

Discussing her writing in an interview, Louise Glück says,

Nothing is more crucial or more exciting than exactness. To be able to say fully and exactly what a thing is—a state of mind, a kind of experience, the significance of two things in a certain kind of relationship—that is getting to the bottom of something. (24)

This desire for exactness is the writer's call or, more accurately, the writer's hook. Caught by the tongue, the writer tries to spit out what isn't liked, dives deeply, trying to shake loose what isn't understood, leaps and flops this way and that until exhausted; still the writer wonders what to do next. Nothing is more exciting than the struggle.

I write a poem called "The Gardener's Pleasure." It starts with the lines, "It's not the flowers / pushing toward the sun / the fruit pulling / its branch into arch." Even though I liked the balance in the push and pull of it all, I change the lines to read, "It's not the flowers / petalling the sun / the fruit pulling / its branch into arch." Bringing back the pleasures of the gardens I have known, I sense that "pushing toward" does not plant the image as well as "petalling." I strike toward that hook of exactness, substituting one word for another, wanting to swallow it all in.

The whole poem reads:

It's not the flowers
petalling the sun,

the fruit pulling
its branch into arch,
or the tomatoes' purple red
or the melons' deep thump.

It's not the shades of green
lush and full after rain
layered into their family portrait.

It's not those leaves
shaped like hands
anticipating prayer,
or the pointed ones
pining for protection.

Nor is it that moment
when ambition comes to light.

It's that dark dirt,
cool and moist, breaking
in your bruised hands,
ready for seed.

I see my desire for exactness not only in my search for just the right word, just the right tone, or just the right sound, but also in my organizing structure, a structure that moves by means of uncovering, stripping away, elimination. Exactness is always a matter of weeding, pulling away this and that, turning over and breaking up what isn't ready, spading. For the gardener's pleasure, like the writer's, comes from digging into those dark places, digging out what might choke or smother, digging deep in preparation for seed. Structurally, I discover what the gardener's pleasure is by recognizing what it is not. I seek a clearing, a place where I can begin to see. I try to point to viable possibilities, only to say, "Not that."

And in the pointing, I add details, layer them into the poem to create a backdrop for what I want to claim is the gardener's pleasure. Pointing is the gesture that asserts "there." It locates, tells the eye where to look. It fingers significance, sometimes with the force of a fist and sometimes with the grace of a good lover's touch. To point is to believe in referents, in the possibility of languaging human life with enough exactness, at least for a moment in time, to allow oneself to rest.

Circling My "Oh's"

Remembering the pleasures of the garden, I am back at my father's house, a nine-year-old boy, digging in a small garden he has given me. It is late in the afternoon and he is finishing his yard work. He stands over me for a moment, seeing how I have prepared the dirt. He looks almost savage, covered in dirt, holding clippings from a bush in one hand and shears in the other. He says, "You've made it ready for seed," and I know in that moment that I've done what I was supposed to do. I've done it for my father. This is a moment of deep celebration and connection, unspoken, a moment still waiting to be written. "The Gardener's Pleasure" is a chip of that demonstrative complex, a piece I was ready to write, although there is no evidence in the poem to suggest my father's presence. My father, my gardener, is an emotional touch point I continually circle, trying to locate him, us, trying to learn our joys and sorrows together, trying to hold us in place. He is a center of my affective life. I am always writing him, even at times when I do not recognize that I am doing so. He is always present, always watching, as I am watching him.

How to Watch Your Father Die

Come when you are called, come quickly,
Rush, come closer, now:

Notice how the muscles weaken, the body slows.
Feel the accumulation of days.

Lean in, listen when he speaks,
Bend to his words.

Accept his wishes—no more soup, a sip of water—
As prayers you can answer.

Sit there, day and night, counting each breath
That struggles to leave his bed.

Look at his hands, still, resting on the sheets.
Rub them and make a small fire.

Forgive those who wash his body with indifference.
Bathe him with your lathered presence.

Check the connected machines, again, again.
Enter through his eyes to the pain.

See the signs in his dead stare.
Keep one eye on the emergency bell.

Start when he is young.

I write this poem in fear that my 85-year-old father will not be around long enough to read this homage in print, even though his health is good, even though I have only the cold facts of actuarial tables working against my desire. Regardless if those lines might be judged good or bad by some discerning critic, they let me wrap myself around that sentiment, around my father. They let me live into him. They are a structural womb, supporting me, nourishing me, preparing me for what is to come. And as such, they allow me some peace. The poem, coming forward to name, holds my feelings in its lines. When it does so, I can slip away. In this sense, T. S. Eliot is right when he asserts that "poetry is not a turning loose of emotion, but an escape from emotion" (10).

But escape never lasts long. Circles leak, crack open, explode. I keep trying to hold my breath, but I cannot. I must breathe in again, purifying what I thought I had. I must breathe out again, contaminating what I thought I understood. In that heavy breathing, I curl around, rub against, slide into. Then I am surrounded, seduced into surrender. I write another poem as a temporary record of attachment when I hear again my father call me forward, asking me to circle the son I am or want to be. And I know with poet Maurya Simon, "Every poem, regardless of its merits, re-enacts the birth of self" (138).

It is a self that is always born reaching. It longs for the nurse and doctor's careful scrutiny, for its parent's approving look, for a glimpse of its fraternal twin. It is always looking over its shoulder. Rolled into its room for viewing, it tries to rest inside the circle of eyes. It cannot. Its parents, Grief and Joy, name it "Today." Its brothers and sisters are known as the days of the week. Come Tomorrow, its circle will form elsewhere.

Looping My "Why's"

Each day carries promise, possibilities. One hot August day, my daughter and I decided to go hiking. Hiking is not something we often do, despite the fact that many wonderful hiking trails are within an easy drive of our home. It was drizzling and humid, and as we drove to the trail we had decided to try, I was having second thoughts. I considered suggesting a movie instead, wanting more than anything else just an opportunity to spend some time with my daughter. But before long, we found the beginning point of the trail, got out of the car, and prepared to walk. Not another person was in sight as the quiet seemed to assert itself. But off we went, and in that oppressive heat, alone, I felt responsible for our safety as she ran up and down slippery rocks without a thought for our footing on narrow trails and broken bridges, for our return. Then, when I wanted nothing more than to be back at our car, I saw a tree— not just any tree, but a tree that made me stop.

The Tree

There is a lesson in that
tree growing in the rocks,
its roots stretching out
to reach dirt, one set
snaking to the side following
the crack of the ledge
and the other set slipping
down more than ten feet
until it found its reward.
Those roots held on
to support perhaps fifty feet
of trunk, branches, leaves
claiming their thin space of sky
through the dark woods.
I stopped with my daughter,
amazed, wanting not to miss
the chance to reach down
beyond rock, to be rooted
in the moment to say
just the right thing.
I wanted her to understand
the miraculous, the will
to live against all odds,
the beauty of thirsty belief.
"Look," I whispered.

In this poem for my daughter, I write my father again. I want to say just the right thing to my daughter, as he always has to me. I want to be the teacher to my daughter that he has been to me. I want my daughter to understand, as my father taught me, the beauty of thirsty belief. My father, who knows when soil is ready for seed, who realizes what it might mean to take root in rock, who keeps calling, is a demanding muse. But in the demand, he offers possibilities, ways of seeing him, ways of seeing me. Poetry, as Yusef Komunyakaa says, "reconnects us to the act of dreaming ourselves into existence. Poetry is an action" (22). I become who I am by writing, over and over again, my father. Reginald Gibbons plots the case this way:

> [A]ll poetry is language that is in some way also about language. Because this is so, all poetry, even the most intimate, is also in some way engaged with our social being, since language is the currency of our being with others. And because all poetry is in some way engaged with our social being, all writing is in some corresponding way a kind of self-making. (204)

Poetry is, then, as poet Mark Cox would have it, "a celebration of the difficulties of selfhood" (22). Poets cannot stop describing themselves to themselves, and that descriptive work is a record of endurance.

To endure is to live with promise, with possibilities. It is to believe, with the weed, in the value of living in a crack in the cement. It is to blossom where no blossoms were expected. It is to say that the world might be made habitable. But such faith often is not enough. Perseverance requires the creative. It calls for improvisational acts in a concrete world. To survive in this dry landscape demands watering from the sweat of the brow, watering again and again, until the ground the poet stands upon is ready for seed.

And in writing "The Tree," I write for my daughter. When I shared it with her, she simply said, "That's nice, Daddy." I do not know if she heard what I was trying to say, but I hope that at some time in her life the poem might provide her a little space in the dark wood, might give her branches to climb, might in some small measure let her grow. I write for our roots, for the sap that circulates within us, for the circles that enclose our time together.

Cupping My "You's"

I cup my father and daughter in my hands. It is as if the three of us are potted together. I have planted us there for viewing, gently, wishing no one any harm. I want them to be glad they are there, nestled with me, to feel free to say how they want their roots to intertwine with mine. Reaching out, we find our nourishment. I believe we will grow together, sharing soil, offering shade, believing in the possibility of bloom. When the sun becomes too harsh, we will water each other with our tears.

And if I am exact enough, emotionally and intellectually complex enough, if I am able to write my father and my daughter, then I have extended my family.

I have gathered together those that share common feelings, that see themselves in a moment of language, that come because I have called, just as my father and daughter have called me. I have taken my turn to speak for the tribe. Such speaking allows for cross-fertilization, creating possibilities to be acted upon, to be discarded. In this cross-breeding, I see myself most clearly. I hear what I want and need to say. I become, with those who come to the calling, cupped together.

Cupping asks for listeners who are willing to hear what must be said. It understands the necessity of languaging our lives. It provides a place where what must be told finds a resonance, an echo. Whether that resonance is called recognition, identification, or empathy, its vibrant presence connects us. Although we may resist, if we come close enough, if we slide into the cup, we will taste what is inside. Cupping asks for listeners who come in to witness, who encourage the stepping into speech. It knows that there are times when we must stand aside and stand beside. It realizes that the cup must always be ready to hold more, that we must never let it spill. Cupping asks for listeners who are willing to act. It gathers together those who believe a better world is possible because language can make things happen. Cupped together, we, the members of the tribe, can envision change.

Lettering It All

Richard Hugo writes:

> Behind several theories of what happens to a poet during the writing of a poem—Eliot's escape from personality, Keats's idea of informing and filling another body, Yeats's notion of the mask, Auden's concept of the poet becoming someone else for the duration of the poem—lies the implied assumption that the self as given is inadequate and will not do. (67)

Hugo, in contrast, speaks on behalf of the self, the self that spends a lifetime struggling to learn that writing is a "slow, accumulative way of accepting one's life as valid" (72), that "writing is a way of saying you and the world have a chance" while simultaneously recognizing that "all art is failure" (72). That desire for exactness, for closure, for opening possibilities with those I love and with those I share a language with keeps me writing in search of myself and offers constant reminders that my task can never be accomplished. It is the search that matters. It is an act of faith. It is a belief in letters.

After the soil is ready for seed, after the planting is done, after everything is staked, I petal toward the sun. I celebrate the glory of blossom. I want everyone to see, to circle around. But the joy of flowering comes to an end. Soon no one stops to look, including myself, and I must shed what I once thought was worth seeing if I am to survive. I must start again. I must get the soil ready for seed. Only then can I be made whole.

Whole

Water rises
when the foot comes down.
When the cold foot lifts,
water swallows
the hole left behind.
There are no soft shoes
on the other foot.
There are no small prints
marking the dead shore.
The same hole beckons
the same empty step.
Twice the river said:

Holes are always
filled with something.

Works Cited

Cox, Mark. "The River." *What Will Suffice: Contemporary American Poets on the Art of Poetry.* Eds. Christopher Buckley and Christopher Merrill, 21–22. Salt Lake City: Gibbs-Smith, 1995.

Eliot, T. S. "Tradition and Individual Talent." *Selected Essays of T. S. Eliot,* 3–11. New York: Harcourt, Brace, 1964.

Gibbons, Reginald. "Poetry and Self-Making." *Poets Teaching Poets: Self and the World.* Eds. Gregory Orr and Ellen Bryant Voigt, 187–206. Ann Arbor: University of Michigan Press, 1996.

Glück, Louise. "An Interview with Louise Glück." Interviewed by Jonathan Farmer. *The Writer's Chronicle* 33 (September 2000): 18–25.

Hugo, Richard. *The Triggering Town: Lectures and Essays on Poetry and Writing.* New York: W. W. Norton, 1979.

Komunyakaa, Yusef. "How Poetry Helps People to Live Their Lives." *American Poetry Review* 28 (September/October 1999): 21–27

Simon, Maurya. "The Birth of Poetry." *What Will Suffice: Contemporary American Poets on the Art of Poetry.* Eds. Christopher Buckley and Christopher Merrill, 138. Salt Lake City: Gibbs-Smith, 1995.

CHAPTER 9

Dialogues of Friends and Lovers: A Poetic Analysis

Dialogue 1

FRIEND 1:   I haven't seen you for a while. How are things?
FRIEND 2:   Good. How about with you?
FRIEND 1:   Fine.
FRIEND 2:   That's great.

POEM: In the looking, we test the cliché.
In the lean, we hear.

Dialogue 2

LOVER 1:   Come sit by me.
LOVER 2:   Are you sure I know you well enough? You're not thinking of any funny business, are you?
LOVER 1:   Stop, silly. Come here. I just want you to sit by me.

POEM: Leaves on the same stem
relax into sweet talk
of tomorrow's dew.

Dialogue 3

FRIEND 1:   Can't you spend some time with me?
FRIEND 2:   I'm sorry. I just can't. I wish I could.
FRIEND 1:   You always have something.
FRIEND 2:   You'll be fine. Don't worry so much.

POEM: Measuring cups cannot measure
the mathematics of care.
They only speak in fractions
until they are themselves.
One cup of minutes weighs
more than a cup of advice.

Dialogue 4

LOVER 1:   I wish you would have called.
LOVER 2:   Sorry.
LOVER 1:   It's just that I was worried about you.
LOVER 2:   I know. I should have called.

POEM: Waiting sags in the slow drag of minutes.
Returning runs with remembering's rush.

Dialogue 5

FRIEND 1:   You got your hair cut.
FRIEND 2:   Yeah. Do you like it?
FRIEND 1:   Yeah.

POEM: Observation without evaluation
seldom finds comfort in a question.

Dialogue 6

LOVER 1:   Honey, do you think I look okay in this?
LOVER 2:   It looks fine on you.
LOVER 1:   Does it make me look fat?
LOVER 2:   No. Not at all.

POEM: The magician's illusion keeps us
from being sawed into two.

Dialogue 7

FRIEND 1:   Do you think you could spare some time and help me this afternoon?

FRIEND 2:   Sure.

FRIEND 1:   Oh, that's great.

FRIEND 2:   What time should I come over?

FRIEND 1:   You are so sweet. Can you come around 2:00?

FRIEND 2:   I'll be there.

POEM: We body into connection,
         turning place
         into womb.

Dialogue 8

LOVER 1:   It drives me crazy when you do that.

LOVER 2:   I don't know why you make such a big deal about it.

LOVER 1:   Because you do it just to aggravate me.

LOVER 2:   Must you always take everything in the worst possible way?

POEM: Shattered glass once understood its shape.
         Anger can too easily find its face.

Dialogue 9

FRIEND 1:   That's not how friends treat friends. Friends don't turn their backs on their friends.

FRIEND 2:   They were just trying to help me.

FRIEND 1:   That's a strange way of helping.

POEM: All balls of twine have a center.
         Unwind,
         find where you began.

Dialogue 10

LOVER 1:   Don't you think I'm entitled to some happiness?

LOVER 2:   Of course you are. What would make you happy?

POEM: The blue jays come to the feeder.
         Only the mourning doves stay.

Dialogue 11

FRIEND 1:   I just love that I can tell you everything.
FRIEND 2:   I feel the same way.

POEM: Pour to replenish.
        Pour until someone spills.

Dialogue 12

LOVER 1:   I'll do the cooking if you'll do the dishes.
LOVER 2:   Fair enough.
LOVER 1:   But you can't complain about what I cook.
LOVER 2:   And you can't complain about how I do the dishes.

POEM: Even cats come
        to accept their training.
        Agreement is tomorrow's comfort.

Dialogue 13

FRIEND 1:   You should come over to the house some time.
FRIEND 2:   That would be lovely. It's just that I've been busy.

POEM: When a hand reaches, take it,
        pull forward. Save
        yourself from quicksand. See
        for the first time
        Christ's wound.

Dialogue 14

LOVER 1:   He's just a good friend. I don't know why you get so upset when-
           ever I want to spend some time with him.
LOVER 2:   It seems like you want to spend more and more time with him.
LOVER 1:   We go way back, and he's having a tough time now.
LOVER 2:   Well, so am I.

POEM: Ropes that tie cannot bind.
        They unravel, thread by thread.
        Lassos are best for circling air.

Dialogue 15

FRIEND 1:   I need you to stand by me on this.
FRIEND 2:   You know I will.

POEM: The fence depends upon its posts.

Dialogue 16

LOVER 1:   Must we be with your family again tonight? Don't get me wrong. I like your family, but I was hoping that . . .
LOVER 2:   You know how Mom is.
LOVER 1:   Yes, but I was hoping that just the two of us could be together tonight. Maybe share a bottle of wine. Fix a little dinner. I don't know, maybe make love.
LOVER 2:   That sounds nice, but we really don't have that choice.

POEM: Roses die when put in blood.

Dialogue 17

FRIEND 1:   I can't believe what we did last night.
FRIEND 2:   I can't believe we are still here to talk about it.
FRIEND 1:   I know. That was something.

POEM: Friendship is born in history.
            Memory is its milk.

Dialogue 18

LOVER 1:   I've been thinking. We're not getting any younger, and maybe we should think about having some kids.
LOVER 2:   I like our lives how they are. I don't want anything to change that.

POEM: The present takes in the future
            as a canary takes in seed,
            as a rattler takes in a rat.

            The future falls into the present
            as buds consider their blooms.

Dialogue 19

Friend 1:	Would you give me a back rub?
Friend 2:	Are you sure that's all you want?
Friend 1:	I thought that was settled.
Friend 2:	I'm always open for renegotiating.

Poem: An ice cube placed in water
raises the level,
floats around, melts.
If needed,
the freezer is always ready.

Dialogue 20

Lover 1:	I just don't think we are working anymore.
Lover 2:	What do you mean, "We're not working?"
Lover 1:	We just don't make each other happy.
Lover 2:	Not happy? What do you expect out of a relationship?
Lover 1:	I don't know, but more than what we have.

Poem: Desire collapses on dream's back.

Dialogue 21

Friend 1:	Are you sorry we did that last night?
Friend 2:	Only if it changes our friendship.
Friend 1:	How can that not change our friendship?
Friend 2:	It only will if we let it. And I don't think we should let it.

Poem: Actions await our stories'
inscription, bodying
its weight in feathers
or stones.

Dialogue 22

LOVER 1:	Where do you see yourself in five years?
LOVER 2:	With you.
LOVER 1:	I mean beyond that.
LOVER 2:	That is what matters. There is little beyond that.

POEM: Commitment works its glue,
          sticking together
          the stuck and the unstuck.

Dialogue 23

FRIEND 1:   What are you doing tonight?
FRIEND 2:   Nothing.
FRIEND 1:   Me too.
FRIEND 2:   Want to come over?
FRIEND 1:   Sure.

POEM: Sand, oyster, pearl.
          Out of nothing,
          a pause,
          a doing.

Dialogue 24

LOVER 1:   I just want to cuddle up and not think about a thing.
LOVER 2:   That's fine with me. It's been some week.
LOVER 1:   I know. I'm ready to just shut down.
LOVER 2:   Me too.

POEM: In the crook of an arm,
          hand beside hand,
          knee over knee,
          under a blanket of sweet silence.

Dialogue 25

FRIEND 1:   We are going to miss you while you're gone.
FRIEND 2:   Thanks. That's so nice of you to say that.
FRIEND 1:   No. I mean it. Things just aren't the same when you're not
            around.
FRIEND 2:   I'll be back before you know it.
FRIEND 1:   As far as I'm concerned, that's not soon enough.

POEM: Absence makes the heart
          revise.
          It writes on a shadow.

Dialogue 26

LOVER 1: I thought we would have this time together. I can't believe you're planning to work. It's Friday night, for God's sake!

LOVER 2: I have to get this done.

LOVER 1: Don't you think about anything else besides work?

LOVER 2: Of course I do. But if we don't have anything planned, I don't see why I shouldn't get my work done.

POEM: Equations indicate the weight
on both sides
of the equal sign.
Energy is always linked to mass.

Dialogue 27

FRIEND 1: I'm a little short. Could you lend me a few bucks?

FRIEND 2: How much do you need?

FRIEND 1: Just enough to get me by until I get paid. Then I'll pay you back.

FRIEND 2: How much is enough to get you by?

POEM: Everyone is counting.
The commerce of obligation
is a sad calculus.

Dialogue 28

LOVER 1: I just don't think we can afford it.

LOVER 2: Just think about how much we'd enjoy it.

LOVER 1: That's not the point.

LOVER 2: Of course it is.

POEM: The dishes and the dish washer,
the chair and the sofa,
the rug and the flooring,
the shrub and the garden,
the tickets and the vacation,
and the this and the that
accumulate until everything
and everyone is full
of emptiness.

Dialogue 29

FRIEND 1: I wish you could understand that I'm sad you're leaving.
FRIEND 2: I do, but you need to understand that this is a great opportunity for me. I want you to be happy for me.

POEM: Leaving's promise is
left's despair.
A road.
A dead end.

Dialogue 30

LOVER 1: Don't you love me enough to let me go?
LOVER 2: No. Don't you love me enough to stay?
LOVER 1: No. I can't.
LOVER 2: I can't either.

POEM: Remembering desire,
love's requirements recoil.
Desire is the heart's nail.

Dialogue 31

FRIEND 1: I wish my partner wasn't so jealous.
FRIEND 2: Me too. I hate feeling like we're cheating.
FRIEND 1: Yeah, just because we want to have lunch together.
FRIEND 2: And I hate the idea of giving up our time together.

POEM: A hand-stitched quilt reveals its flaws.
We hide under our holy
and stolen cover.

Dialogue 32

LOVER 1: Do I have any food in my teeth?
LOVER 2: Yes. Right there.
LOVER 1: Why didn't you tell me?
LOVER 2: I didn't notice.
LOVER 1: You never notice anything about me.
LOVER 2: When you asked, I noticed that you have food in your teeth.

LOVER 1:	That's just what I mean—I have to ask.
LOVER 2:	From now on, I'll look at your teeth right after you eat.
LOVER 1:	That's not my point and you know it.
LOVER 2:	Would you please go get the food out of your teeth? It's very distracting.
LOVER 1:	Fine.

POEM:	If the bell rings, then sparring.
	If sparring, then a blow.
	If a blow, then a bruise.
	If a bruise, then evidence.
	If evidence, then a case.
	If a case, then divorce.

Dialogue 33

FRIEND 1:	I can't understand how you could vote for that guy.
FRIEND 2:	At least he isn't a crook, like your man.
FRIEND 1:	I'll take a crook whose views I agree with over someone who believes the crap he does.

POEM:	Startled beyond assumptions,
	they vote on each other's differences
	and find themselves
	wanting.

Dialogue 34

LOVER 1:	I need some space.
LOVER 2:	It seems to me you've carved quite a bit of space between us. You're never around anymore.
LOVER 1:	I've got a lot on my mind.
LOVER 2:	And it's clear that I'm not part of what's on your mind.
LOVER 1:	I didn't say that.
LOVER 2:	I did.

POEM:	When the line drawn in the sand
	washes away,
	the sea still remembers.
	Waste will kill the water.

Dialogue 35

FRIEND 1:   How sweet of you to think of me while you were away!
FRIEND 2:   Oh, it's just a little something I thought you might enjoy.
FRIEND 1:   I will. I just love it.

POEM: On the mantel
a reminder of being
carried away
when you didn't know
you had left.

Dialogue 36

LOVER 1:   Let's make love.
LOVER 2:   Not tonight. Okay?

POEM: Making your presence large
as tragedy, you ask again. You leave
feeling angry, small
as the word no.

Dialogue 37

FRIEND 1:   Remember when we first met?
FRIEND 2:   Yeah. I thought you were an ass.
FRIEND 1:   And I thought the same about you.
FRIEND 2:   Maybe that's how we connected.

POEM: Two asses,
moving together in the night,
stalking their shadow.

Dialogue 38

LOVER 1:   Even after all these years, there is still no one I would rather spend
my time with.
LOVER 2:   We do work well together.
LOVER 1:   I'd say it's been a great fit.
LOVER 2:   Me too.

POEM: For the machinery to run,
oil the parts.

Dialogue 39

FRIEND 1: Can you show me how to do that?
FRIEND 2: Sure. It's really easy.

POEM: A slow bow.
A shaping look.

Humility's hand is asking's answer.

Dialogue 40

LOVER 1: What did the doctor say?
LOVER 2: We won't know anything until the results of the tests are back.
LOVER 1: When will that be?
LOVER 2: Early next week.

LOVER In the waiting, the unsaid.
In the idle, the imagination.
In the anticipation, plans.
In the moment, feeble care.

Dialogue 41

FRIEND 1: What he said was just mean-spirited.
FRIEND 2: I know. I was surprised that he would say such a thing.
FRIEND 1: It's not like him at all.
FRIEND 2: I wonder if there is more to the story than we know.
FRIEND 1: I've heard some things.
FRIEND 2: What?

POEM: A puzzle awaits its picture
in the pleasure
of its production.

Dialogue 42

LOVER 1: What are you going to get me for my birthday?
LOVER 2: I don't know. What do you want?
LOVER 1: I want you to surprise me.
LOVER 2: Then why did you ask what I was getting you?

POEM: The burden of getting it
         right demands
         knowing how to play.

Dialogue 43

FRIEND 1:   Is Chris still doing that?
FRIEND 2:   Yes.
FRIEND 1:   You don't have to put up with it.
FRIEND 2:   I don't see what I can do about it.

FRIEND   Knowing you'll have to step
          in the same river
          more than twice,
          you lift, up and down,
          your weighted boots.

Dialogue 44

LOVER 1:   I want you all to myself. I want to gobble you up.
LOVER 2:   Sorry, I'm only edible on Tuesdays.

POEM: Tease turns to taunt
         in food fights.

Dialogue 45

FRIEND 1:   What sounds can you imitate?
FRIEND 2:   You mean like a cow or a car crash?
FRIEND 1:   Yeah. Have I ever done my cat in heat for you?

POEM: Silly
         laughter is louder
         than the cat's night shriek.

Dialogue 46

LOVER 1:   Go play golf.
LOVER 2:   Are you sure?
LOVER 1:   Yes. I have plenty to do around here.

POEM: Permission is a deep nod,
          a goodbye kiss,
          a waving hand.

Dialogue 47

FRIEND 1:   Thanks for calling me back.
FRIEND 2:   Sure. What's up?

POEM: Positioned, ready
          as the runner anticipating
          the gun.

Dialogue 48

LOVER 1:   Should we add that to our collection?
LOVER 2:   Well, it's expensive but it does complete the set.
LOVER 1:   It would be nice to have.
LOVER 2:   Let's buy it. Okay?

POEM: Collecting each other
          in the memory
          of the buy.

Dialogue 49

FRIEND 1:   Let's play catch.
FRIEND 2:   Sure.

POEM: Until one is too low, too high, or too wide
          back and forth
          the communicative toss.

Dialogue 50

LOVER 1:   I love you.
LOVER 2:   And I love you.

POEM: Unspoken qualifiers
          hug the heart,
          squeeze until there is
          a letting go.

CHAPTER 10

Always Dying: Living between *Da* and *Fort*

Da.

There. I will reach for the moment, trying to hold on. I will reach for the moment, working it with my fingers, turning it, squeezing it, feeling it. I will hold it as one might grasp a bird, sensing its racing heartbeat and keeping it secure, firm between my hands. I will see that I cannot. I will be reaching forever, trying to hold on. I will hold my breath. I will know, with poet Tim Shea, that "to write / is to let death / in" (45). I will always write in grief for what is lost. Always. Already. Gone.

Fort.

Gone. Freud's grandson understood power when, by tugging on a piece of string, he pulled his wooden reel into visibility and when, by letting go, he let it slide into invisibility. But presence and absence aren't always matters of choice. Too often strings are cut, out of our control, or become entangled. He understood too the pleasure of repetition, pulling on the string again and again to relive the moment. But repeating isn't always a matter of doing again. Too often repetition is a representation of what cannot be accomplished twice. There.

Da.

There. The show had been running for months—a success. Each night the audience would come, filled with anticipation, energized, prepared by reports of the show's wonder and poised to listen. The actors too would come, each night a little less excited. Nothing you could mark from night to night but something that began to show over time. The show became ordinary, as familiar as the "How are you?" accompanying a handshake. Lines were spoken without thinking. Movements were completed by habit. Exits were made either too quickly or too slowly. The show would start. They would do their parts. The show would end. Ready for it to be over, they stopped doing a second curtain call. The show closed a week later. Gone.

Fort.

Gone. I hadn't heard from my old college roommate in over thirty years. Shortly after graduation, we lost contact. He married, joined the navy, and went to Japan; I married, took my chances with the draft, and went to Vietnam. The war separated us as if we were naughty children, and indeed, there were times when we were. So when my second wife said she received an e-mail from an old friend of mine asking if she was related to me, I smiled, thinking about those wonderful college days when we just didn't know any better. We exchanged e-mails for a few weeks, asking about old friends, new wives, and children. I learned that he is a manager of several convenience stores in the Dallas/Fort Worth area. I told him that if he was ever coming my way to please stop by. He wrote the same. Neither of us have done so. There.

Da.

There. David Ignatow's poem "Two Friends" tells us where we stand. In his short poem, one friend announces to the other "I'm dying" and the other responds with perfunctory clichés. There is no sympathy, no compassion. There is no embrace. Within a few moments, the friend escapes. Gone.

Fort.

Gone. I'm not sure when I began to bore him. I'm sure I didn't at first. We cut our academic teeth together, thinking through disciplinary arguments, considering departmental politics, writing together with passion. Together, we consulted. Together, we went to conventions. Together, we played golf. Together, we drank. Together, we talked about our wives. Together, we lived our lives. So when did it happen? Perhaps it began when I joined him for a week on his sabbatical and I talked of his return. Maybe such talk told him he had to leave. Perhaps it began when his health seemed to fail, when the doctors prescribed pills after pills in their ongoing guessing game, never quite finding the correct diagnosis. Maybe I just didn't know what to say. Perhaps it began when he left his wife. Maybe he did not want to insist on allegiance at a time when he needed just that. Perhaps it began when he first started giving me gifts—books I might like, ties I might enjoy, wines I might try. Maybe these were parting gestures, wrapped in guilt. Whenever it began, it came quickly and I was pathetic. In his presence, my talk felt tedious as he would rush the conversation to an end. My stories seemed empty and pointless, as he nodded as if he had heard them all before. I watched him seek others for their company and I felt hurt. Now he has moved away, but he remains here, a ghost, untouchable. There.

Da.

There. I have stood alongside Tobias in Edward Albee's *A Delicate Balance* and felt that years of friendship must account for something and felt too that only when asked what my limits might be would I recognize the hollowness of my belief. So when friends make demands, I try not to say no but, like Tobias, I do not want their terrors, their plagues. I accept them only so that my life isn't a lie. I say with Tobias: "I like you fine; I find my liking you has limits. . . . But those are my limits! Not yours!" And like Harry, when my terrors and my plagues are upon me, I wonder if I am loved enough to take them to someone else's house. Gone.

Fort.

Gone. I cannot pull them up in my mind. Their names I remember, but they are names without faces. So when I was invited to my thirtieth high school reunion, I did not go. I could not see myself looking around the room without images to connect to names. I could not see myself standing in that cool courtyard, shaded by those ivy-covered building, talking again as I did those many years ago. I could not see myself sitting in Mr. Montgomery's classroom again, afraid to speak, afraid I might get it wrong. I could not see myself not wanting to hold her hand, to pick up where we had left off, to wonder what would have happened if. I see her clearly. There.

Da.

There. Usually he ate to live. He surely was no food connoisseur, but he knew he was in the presence of something special when he put the first morsel in his mouth. When she handed him the blueberry muffin he'd chosen, she seemed pleased by his pick. A quick smile came, and she said, "I hope you enjoy it," as if she already knew the verdict was accomplished in the selection. He peeled the paper from its sides and felt that it was still warm. He broke off a piece. It was moist and covered by a thin crust that crunched on first bite but began to melt in his mouth. The blueberries, full and dark, had a slight tang. He quickly took another bite. Standing behind the counter, she smiled again and turned to her chores, knowing he would be back. He pulled off another piece and ate, then another, and another. The blueberry muffin was gone. Gone.

Fort.

Gone. When the love between them left is hard to say. Perhaps it left with the accumulation of annoyances or perhaps as the love died, everything began to annoy—his aggravating snoring, his unreasonable demands, his predictable self-righteousness and her compulsive cleaning, her excessive buying, her negative judgments. Whenever it happened, it happened as a slow complaint that rubbed against them both, a complaint that was never spoken. They lived, day in and day out, watching each other as two animals might circle prey, ready to pounce but afraid the prey might be more than can be handled. There.

Da.

There. The opening kiss in the film *Kids* terrifies with its intimacy. The camera offers a close-up of two young bodies, passionate in embrace, turning this way and that, pushing, sucking, tonguing. You see their heads, together, filling the screen, magnified. You hear their sloppy noises. You see their eyes closed, then searching. You see their spit. You see them wanting. You see them forever. You see sex. You are embarrassed and want to look away but you don't. You are fascinated. You remember what you learned in your film theory class. You imagine that if the kiss would go on for a moment longer, they would begin to devour each other, bit by bit, until only a pair of worn lips would remain. Gone.

Fort.

Gone. When does it leave a relationship? When does it lose its power? When does it not matter anymore? When does it carry so much hard history that it just doesn't seem worth it? When does it seem too much like a chore, like something that has to get done? When does it repeat itself, the same time, the same place, the same hands? When does it become a couple's cancer? When does it become negotiated in silence? When does it stay, clinging like an old fragrance? There.

Da.

There. James Bond always knows just what to say. He never struggles for just the right word, never pauses too long before he speaks, never talks too softly to be heard. Even when he might get it wrong, he knows just how to make amends. He is the perfect man, handsome, strong, smart. Dry martini in hand, he eliminates evil. Dry martini in hand, he makes love. Bond is 007 cool, or so he was before history had its way. Gone.

Fort.

Gone. When all is said and done, the hero turns his back on us and leaves. Alone, he rides into the sunset or he turns from the carnage, perhaps with just a trickle of blood running down his thigh. There is no standing around for applause. He does not linger to see what might be said about his virtue or to gather what might be his rewards. He just leaves, noble, independent, confident in the wisdom of his actions. The hero never second-guesses. He lives so that he might return again, ready to act in the name of justice, in the name of those too weak to fend for themselves, in the name of eye-for-an-eye laws that we are too afraid to change. There.

Da.

There. The note left on the counter read: "I've gone to the store. I'll be back soon." She never returned. He drank cup after cup of Constant Comment spice tea. Gone.

Fort.

Gone. Child actors never die; they just grow older. They lose their curls, their cute smiles, their charm, and before you know it, they're chewing scenes in search of what got left behind. That's when the parts usually stop coming. A few make it to the other side, but most live scrapbook lives, always looking back, always listening for their cue. There.

Da.

There. For fourteen years, I have traveled to present my parents with their only granddaughter. Twice a year, over Christmas and summer vacations, we would appear, expecting them to be sitting around their cluttered dining-room table in their straightback chairs, playing cards, working puzzles, preparing food, reading the paper. We would join them around that table until our backs, more accustomed to the softness of sofas, would complain. We would join them for the pleasure of the moment, knowing how the candy dish had been filled with our favorite chocolates, how the beds were made and turned down, how the house was decorated with Santas peeking around every corner or was made fresh with summer flowers. We would join them for the comfort of their company and for the chance to connect. I would watch them, watch them hard, as they grew older, and they would watch their granddaughter turn into a young woman. They would know but would not hear her say, "Are we going back this summer?" Gone.

Fort.

Gone. He decided that as far as he was concerned, his son was dead. At that moment, he felt relief. He simply said to himself, "He's not my responsibility any longer. I did what I could." He repeated the words, listening carefully to what he was saying. He said them again, convincing himself he was right. That night his son came to him in a dream, stabbing him, over and over, with the family name. There.

Da.

There. Villains often meet their just ends with death. We applaud as the world regains its order. For we are the townspeople who move to the side when the shoot-out is to begin, the shoppers who dodge the recklessness of the car chase, the frightened hostages who wait to be rescued. We can produce a needed scream, drop a tear or two, or provide a backdrop for a scene. We are the witnesses that everything has returned to its rightful place. Sometimes that requires death, even our own. Gone.

Fort.

Gone. The first time he saw the show, he was ecstatic. Usually slow in gesture and mood, he rocked with the remembered sounds and his hands fluttered praise. He could not be contained. "You have to see it! You have to see it!" he exclaimed to everyone who would listen. The next time he saw it, he watched in quiet awe. His concentration was deep and focused, and when it ended he shook his head, marveling. His was an act of veneration, of the devout standing before his god. There can be little surprise, then, that the third time he saw it, he brought his daughter, obligated as a parent to provide religious education. His pleasure came with her conversion. Now they sing the lyrics together each day on the way to school in loud, joyful sounds that echo around the neighborhood like prayers. There.

Da.

There. I'm not sure how it starts, maybe a bruised ego, maybe a bad decision or two, maybe from the arrogance of all concerned, but I know I don't want it in my house, the "he saids" and the "she saids," the maneuvering, the calculating, the counting of votes, the closed doors. Politics are too political. It works on you from the inside, and insiders are too close to the heart of the matter. It saddens. It angers. It takes and takes and returns nothing. It devours as it goes. The heart of the matter is empty. Gone.

Fort.

Gone. How many dead bodies might I count? The evening news might show me two or three on any given night. The cop shows that follow might present me with several more. I might add up the bodies from the funerals of friends, acquaintances, and relatives. One Shakespeare play might give me half a dozen or so. A Stallone or Eastwood film might top a hundred. I might name those I knew in Vietnam who did not return. The pictures from massacres and lynchings might total in the hundreds. Those comic book and cartoon deaths might be added. I might figure in that teenage army prisoner who died of an overdose while I tried to assist the doctors' desperate efforts. The victims of natural disasters might compute into the thousands. Newspaper accounts of car wrecks, suicides, and murders might average five to ten a day. Bodies from diseases—plagues, heart attacks, cancer—might account for many more. I might list them all, all the dead bodies I have seen, one after another, and I might count my own. There.

Da.

There. No, she doesn't look like herself. She looks like a figure from a wax museum, placed for viewing for the visitors to stroll passed. She is frozen, lifeless. You recognize who the figure is supposed to be but it's off just a little here and there—the cheeks too puffy, the eyebrows too dark, the lips too pale—just enough to let you know that it's not right. That's why wax museums are such frightening places. They trade in possession when they have nothing to possess. Like now, with her, she is nowhere to be found. Gone.

Fort.

Gone. Dying in performance is an art. We are at our best when death is violent—the bullet flinging the body back, the sword slicing the body from the head, the knife cutting the throat, the grenade separating limbs. We can make blood spurt, pour, or puddle from a wound. We can even show the fear the moment before death arrives. We are less skilled when we have to die in a loved one's arms. We never get right how the body drops down into dead weight, how the eyes open, shocked by the finality of it all, and how those still living turn from the corpse. There.

Da.

There. The obituaries. Each day they are listed and each day I meet them differently. Sometimes they are pictured, their importance marked by the column inch. Sometimes they are a page to skip. Sometimes they are a semantic lesson in the cruelty of naming. Sometimes they are a mathematical equation predicting probable time left. Sometimes they are a nervous read. Sometimes they are stories of fathers or mothers who have graduated from this or that school, who have spent the weight of their years working here or there, who have left others behind. Sometimes they are instructions—services at such-and-such funeral home, burial at such-and-such cemetery, no flowers. Sometimes they are children, single-digit young. Always though, they are passings without explanation, and each day curiosity pulls me to the messiness of their deaths, to the failure of their bodies, to the pain of their flesh. I am grateful my curiosity is never satisfied. Necrology. Necrotomy. Necrosis. Gone.

Fort.

Gone. When the credits begin to roll, most of the audience begins to leave. Only some additional attraction—outtakes, a theme song, a continuing image—might hold them in the aisle, glancing back over their shoulders. They don't need a list of names to decide if credit is or is not due. But a few will remain seated, straining to see the names of copyists, set-production assistants, best boys, and grips between the moving bodies trying to depart. They read to connect; they read for recognition. There.

Da.

There. In *The Writing Life*, Annie Dillard advises:

> Write as if you are dying. At the same time, assume you write for an audience consisting solely of terminal patients. That is, after all, the case. What would you begin writing if you knew you would die soon? What could you say to a dying person that would not enrage by its triviality? (68)

Who can speak in the face of such a mandate? Gone.

Fort.

Gone. She understood it to be a hallowed space. She knew that the theatre held, rumbling in the rafters and riding the rigging, all the voices that were ever present. She had added her own and stopped to listen on closing night after everyone had gone. At first all she heard was the silence, but she waited, listening, still. Then she heard something else. Perhaps it was just the wind; perhaps it was her mind playing tricks. But she swore that the theatre spoke: "Prayers," it whispered, "prayers." There.

Da.

There. It is all about loss. Everything is dying. First there was God, then the author, and now the subject. All that is left is an inaccessible is. Everything slips away. Theatre, Peggy Phelan tells us in *Mourning Sex*, is a "response to a psychic need to rehearse for loss, and especially for death" (3). The perpetual disappearance of theatrical acts teaches us how to mourn what is no longer present. It teaches us that to represent can only result in loss, that there is no holding on. This lesson never settles. We resist it when we speak, when we write, when we listen. We never get it right. There is only the coming and going, only the space between. Tears mark the spot. Always already. Everything evaporates. Only stains and shadows remain. Ghosts. Gone.

Fort.

Works Cited

Albee, Edward. *A Delicate Balance: A Play*. New York: Plume, 1997.
Dillard, Annie. *The Writing Life*. New York: HarperCollins, 1998.
Ignatow, David. "Two Friends." *Figures of the Human*. Middleton, CT: Wesleyan University Press, 1964.
Phelan, Peggy. *Mourning Sex: Performing Public Memories*. Boston: Routledge, 1997.
Shea, Tim. "Scratched into the Tree of Original Sin's Bark." *American Poetry Review* 26 (1997): 45.

CHAPTER 11

The Academic:
An Ethnographic Case Study

Integrating into the Culture

He came to the academy from the golf course, boasting a scratch handicap; drives, with their slight draw, that ran and ran; and a putting touch that big men just weren't suppose to have. He was also the owner of many wonderful unread books and a GPA that was clear evidence of where he was spending his time (1.8, 1.69, 1.32, and 2.0 for his first two years in college, to be exact). He had gone, scholarship in hand, to Southern Methodist University to play golf in the Southwest Conference, the best conference for golf during 1960s. There was little doubt in his mind that he would become a pro, perhaps not of the caliber of Arnold Palmer, his boyhood idol, but good enough to play on tour.

Along the way, he encountered Ms. Willis, a dark-haired, middle-aged, 4'8" woman who took the teaching of the universitywide required course, The Nature of Man, quite seriously. Even though he had made solid C's on the two previous examinations, it seemed that Ms. Willis objected to how frequently he attended her class. When he arrived to take the final examination, she came at his 6'3" tanned body, pointing her finger right at him and yelling, "I dare you come in here to take this exam. Get out of my room. Get out." He left and had enough time to get in an extra nine holes.

In between rounds, he had to select a major. He tried English first but found all the red marks on his papers just too depressing. Besides, all that reading they wanted him to do seemed a bit much. So on the good council of a golf buddy who said that it was easy and all the classes were filled with chicks, he tried sociology. It was a happy union until he had to go to this professor's house for a class meeting and he managed to walk through the sliding-glass window. He remembers looking down at a plate of food he could not identify when his knee and head hit the glass simultaneously. After it shattered, he was still standing there, looking down at his food, blood coming from his forehead and knee, still wondering what it was and saying, "Oh, thank you. No, I don't need another plate. I don't think much glass got in there." He never quite felt comfortable around the sociology department after that.

After that, he worked harder on his short game. He knew he could cut a shot a round off his score if he could get better around the greens. That work as well as years of work since he was twelve years old paid off—he played either the first or second man on the team during his first two years of school and he won most of his matches. The coach was so impressed that he offered him a job in the pro shop for the summer. His life, he thought, was falling into place. This, he believed, was his first step as a professional golfer. There was only one problem: he hated it, hated the long hours of watching other people play when he couldn't, hated the country-club set that treated the staff with little or no respect, and hated the life he saw unfolding before him.

So there he was, knee-high in the rough, searching. He felt like he had grounded his club in the sand, like he had hit a shot out of bounds when he was one up with one to go, like he had shanked an easy wedge on the last hole at Augusta. He ended that summer like a lost ball and rolled into Speech 101, where he gave his first speech on how to swing a golf club to an instructor, Dr. Lee Roloff, who saw in him something more than a golfer. How he did so, he'll never know. All he knew was that he liked hearing him talk and after taking twenty-one hours under his instruction, he was graduating as a double major in sociology and speech communication. Having discovered that thinking could be as much fun as hooking a one-iron around a tree, he decided to pursue a master's, not the coat, but the degree. He pursued still more hours under Roloff's instruction, taken on a probationary status because of his undergraduate grades. In the middle of his program of study he made an unplanned visit to Vietnam but returned to complete the degree and landed his first teaching position at Virginia Polytechnic Institute and State University, a university that did not have its own golf course.

He arrived at Virginia Tech with his master's in hand, loads of books whose spines were not broken, and questions still lingering in his head about whether this is what he wanted to do with his life. He arrived knowing nothing. His job was to teach four speech courses a semester and to help develop a speech communication major.

He filled out all the paperwork at payroll, signed up for the health plan that seemed best, and found a place to live. He arranged his office: he put the few file folders he had in the new file drawers they provided; he decided that hanging one's diploma should be left to medical doctors; he sharpened his pencils. He got to work on the syllabi for the courses he would be teaching and soon had accomplished that task. Then, much to his dismay, he looked around and realized he had no idea what he should do next. It was 10:00 in the morning the week before school was scheduled to begin and he didn't know how to fill his time. He felt, well, rather pointless. Others seemed to be scurrying around, busy as he had assumed he would be. He wondered what academics did with their time.

But he was officially a part of the Department of Performing Arts and Communications, a department that housed speech communication, theatre, and music, a department that would grow from six faculty members when he started in 1971 to thirty-three faculty when he left in 1974 to pursue his doctorate at the University of Illinois. This growth was the most solid proof that Virginia Tech had a desperate desire to build a reputation as more than an agricultural college. It was also a university with a desperate desire to be considered among the nation's best; in its desire it established tenure and promotion standards that few could meet: a book, about ten well-placed articles, several grants, supporting book reviews, conference presentations, workshops, etc. Meanwhile, he was getting up his nerve to submit his first paper to the Southern Speech Communication Association convention.

Standing against the wall in the lobby of his first convention hotel, he watched people greet one another with open arms and deep hugs. He saw people who seemed to know everyone. He looked on as others tried to slip away to dinner before their group got too big. He didn't know anyone. After a while, he returned to his room, ordered room service, and read again the longest paper, besides his thesis, he had ever written. It was ten pages. He argued in his paper, "An Integrated Program of Communication Exercises," that certain communication principles can be effectively taught when strategized as a series of exercises. Most of the paper described the exercises. He was surprised following his presentation that the audience wanted to question him about whether exercises borrowed from humanistic psychology were appropriate for a communication classroom. He was surprised how spirited the discussion became. He was surprised there were questions. He returned to Virginia Tech sensing he had gone through some sort of initiation rite but wasn't sure what to make of it.

He returned to the classroom and taught, without adequate training, a wide range of speech communication courses: public speaking, oral interpretation, small group communication, persuasion, public relations, argumentation and debate, and interpersonal communication. Despite being most prepared to teach oral interpretation, the course that captured his imagination was interpersonal communication. Perhaps it was because he was going through a divorce at the time. He felt that he could make a difference in students' lives, that Carl Rogers, Abraham Maslow, and William Schutz couldn't possibility be wrong, that he could share the wisdom of his twenty-five years. On most weekends, he held encounter groups in his home.

And so after three years of training on the job, he thought he wanted to stay in the academy. That meant, of course, that he would have to switch sides of the desk in the pursuit of his doctorate. He didn't anticipate any problems. He was on top of the interpersonal literature, he knew the field of oral interpretation, and he had decided on his dissertation topic—poetry therapy—a subject that would allow him to combine his love for both interpersonal and oral interpretation. Or so he thought.

Still Integrating

On the first day he met with his advisor, Dr. Joanna Maclay, he mentioned that he wanted to target his coursework toward a dissertation on poetry therapy. She listened and then, while cleaning her corncob pipe on the spike of one of her heels, said, "Now hon, you don't really want to do that, now do you?" Her argument was persuasive. He was convinced he had made a mistake. On the first day of class, he went to Dr. Jesse Delia's course on interpersonal communication. He could not find Rogers, Maslow, or Schutz. He could not find anything that looked even remotely familiar. He joked after being handed a thirty-page bibliography about whether the assignment was to read the bibliography. Still, on that first day of class, he went to Dr. Maclay's Interpretation of Southern Fiction course. The literary study model of performance, he was told, was the model preferred for the course. He did not know that there was more than one model, and he didn't think the one he knew was the literary study one. His confidence dried up quicker than White Out.

This was the beginning of how his doctoral program began to do its work. By spring semester of his first year, he was sure he would never complete the degree. He knew he wasn't smart enough. He didn't read quickly enough, he didn't follow arguments that were presented in class, he didn't ask insightful questions. He thought all of his classmates were doing much better than he. He took to wearing a denim, broad-rimmed hat pulled down to just over his eyes. He became quiet, sullen. He worried about his mental health. But his doctoral program was a success. After five years, he graduated convinced he didn't know a thing.

He landed a job at Wayne State University, based in part on the strength of an article he published with the help of Dr. Maclay. She articulated the thesis of the piece, clarified the arguments, provided the literary examples to make the case, pointed out relevant scholarship, gave detailed editorial assistance, and offered her encouragement, and he published his first single-authored essay. He still thinks of that article as one of the best he has ever written.

His department at Wayne State was large, including such areas of study as communication disorders, journalism, rhetoric and communication theory, theatre, and oral interpretation. It was so large, in fact, that the faculty as a whole never met together and, in some cases, were never introduced to each other. Like the faculty associated with many metropolitan campuses, professors seldom did their work on campus. After teaching their classes and holding their office hours, they were gone. Day after day, he would make the long walk from his office to main departmental office, reading the nameplates of faculty he had never seen. He was one of a few departmental faculty who liked spending their working time at the office. He discovered that his preference matched his students' preference.

He was also one of three faculty in the oral interpretation area. One had been on a temporary line for several years and left a year after he arrived. They never seemed to develop much of a relationship, perhaps because she had applied for the permanent line but was not interviewed for the position. Despite that tension, he threw himself into his work. The job gave him his first taste of graduate-level education, a taste he has continued to enjoy. He savored the challenge of it. He fed on the anticipation of questions, the hard work of preparation, the exhaustion at the end of a seminar. These were his days of apprenticeship, modeled on his previous teachers. These were the days when he became sure that this was what he wanted to do with his life. These were the days when he felt he had entered the academy. Still, he didn't know if he belonged.

While at Wayne State, he was never sure if it was appropriate to ask the chair a question he might have. When he accepted another job at Southern Illinois University, he made an appointment. He started the conversation by simply saying, "I've taken another job." "Would more money keep you here?" the chair responded. "No," was his reply, but he thought he might have stayed if the chair had given him some indication that he was appreciated before he was ready to walk out the door, if the department had some spirit of a scholarly community, if Wayne State had not been in the heart of Detroit.

Cultural Immersion

Having decided the academy was where he wanted to be, he heard the tenure clock ticking for the first time. The official standards were clear: publish about six substantive articles, teach well enough not to generate complaints, and take on some university and professional service. The one criterion that was just as real but never a part of any formal document was collegiality. He knew that it mattered if the faculty wanted him around. He refused, however, to kowtow to anyone or play the sycophant just for the sake of tenure. He would, he decided, just say what he thought and do his work. He made enemies.

Nothing saddened him more. He never intended to give offense. He didn't want to be unkind or contentious and he didn't like being at war. Often he felt that he had done nothing wrong—he simply represented something that someone else could not abide. He asked friends what he should do, tried to straighten out what he thought were misunderstandings, and had long talks with the chair of the department. At its worst, he felt like someone was hitting him in the head with a sand wedge. In his sixth year, he received the unanimous support for tenure from the faculty, save one, even though he counted two tenured faculty members who he believed wished he wasn't around. One would retire soon, he thought, and the other he would just avoid. He was soon to learn, however, that avoidance is a difficult strategy. Nothing, he discovered, requires more time than the negotiation of faculty egos.

And time was in short supply. He wondered how academics managed to do what they do with so little time. He wanted more time to teach; to answer phone messages; to grade; to prepare for class; to meet with students; to write; to cooperate with local high schools and community colleges; to direct productions; to propose new courses; to take classes; to construct preliminary examination questions and evaluate the answers when written; to revise the curriculum; to support the department's student organizations; to attend professional meetings; to send and answer e-mail; to place book orders; to keep current with the latest technology; to research; to develop co-curricular workshops and lecture series; to perform; to write letters of recommendation; to read; to attend honors day, graduation ceremonies, tributes, award presentations and banquets; to find a word in the dictionary; to advise students' research reports, theses, and dissertations; to write grant proposals; to straighten the office; to review articles for scholarly journals; to recruit new students; to file; to serve the community; to submit reports; to sit on departmental, college, university, and professional committees; to have a beer with a colleague; and so on. He had difficulty establishing priorities. The job seemed to push him around, demanding that he do this or that before he realized where his time had gone.

Still, he came to school every day, often before the secretarial staff, and stayed until well after they left. He kept plugging away, even though his list of things he feels he should have finished before now never ends. That has always been his strength—a willingness to put in the hours. Perhaps he learned to do so long ago on the driving range, hitting ball after ball until his hands bled.

But he knew then, as he does now, that putting in the hours may not be enough. He wishes he were more capable, more articulate, smarter.

He remembers the time he chaired the business meeting of the Performance Studies Division of the National Communication Association in Miami. Over the years, he had watched a number of people move the meeting along with efficiency and skill. The task did not seem that difficult. He had a simple agenda to get through. He just had to call on several committee chairs and to make a few announcements. But once he began the meeting, nothing went right: he lost his place, he mumbled, he couldn't remember what to do. When he tried to read the list of announcements, he couldn't read what he had written. He was incompetent, disabled by apprehension. He was, to say the least, embarrassed. Afterward, he walked alone on the beach, wondering if he could return.

He remembers the years he spent trying to write about performance as a method. He believed, perhaps more strongly than he should have, that the field needed a detailed discussion of that subject. He thought no issue was more pressing, more worthy of his attention. He wrote theoretical essays, survey articles, and production-based pieces. He wrote and he wrote and he wrote some more. He wrote until he was too discouraged to write anymore. He wrote until he failed. He finally became convinced that he could not write a persuasive piece on the topic. He could not make a sufficient rhetorical case for the reviewers. They were kind but dismissive. Yet he still believes in what he was trying to say. His failure, he thinks, was rhetorical. His failure, he knows, was ability.

He remembers the productions that never quite worked, one in particular where he and his cast never clicked. He wanted a show they refused to do. He wanted their love for a text they did not appreciate. He wanted a performance style they resisted. In the end nothing worked, not even the pleasures of coming together to try to make art. All left glad it was over. No one learned. No one grew closer.

He remembers too many classes that didn't come together, classes where students would rather sleep in than hear his lecture, where students would do what they were told but really didn't care, where students weren't touched. The student who yawned loudly while he was making a key point and the student who left the classroom while he was leading an important discussion stay in his mind. These students are unsettling as they rub against moments of success. They have power. They are humbling correctives to arrogance.

But, all in all, he has no regrets, although, as he approached fifty, he did consider what it might take to get his game back in shape and pursue the Senior Tour. It was nothing more than a fun fantasy; he likes where he is, likes the choice he made. Of course, there are things he would change, but most of those things are things in him. He wishes he were more capable, more articulate, smarter. Yet he manages. He does what he has to do and what he can do. He has even said to his daughter, a high-schooler who has visions of a theatre career, that the academic life is one she might want to consider. He said to her, "Despite the complaints you might have heard at home, the academy has no limits. It is a place where you can discover how good you are."

Reflecting Culture

Every once in a while a graduate student or a beginning assistant professor might look at him and think, "There's someone who made it in the academy." But he knows better. He knows there is no making it. Even after a golf round of three under, there are things that need work. One can never be satisfied. There is always more to do—another article to write, another class to teach, another book to read. That's what he likes—there is no winning, no possibility of mastery, no chance for merit. His strongest desire after learning that he had received tenure was to show the faculty who had supported him that they had not made a mistake.

Culture is not static; it is an ongoing process of social construction, ever changing, always in negotiation. But if one were to freeze just the right moment, he would be standing there, perhaps not in the center, but there, in the academic culture, smiling and frowning, glad to be a part of it all. With the door of his office wide open, he is moving to his desk now, ready for another day. He will unpack his bag, look around, and assess what needs to be done. He will make a list that he will not get through.

He still goes out and plays a round of golf every now and then. But more often than not, he would rather be writing or teaching. He would rather fret until he found just the right verb than cut a four-wood around a dogleg; he would rather watch the complexity of a sentence grow than sink a fifty-footer; he would rather feel the pleasure of completing an essay than drink to a par round on the nineteenth hole. He would rather be building to the climax of a class lecture just before the hour is to end than holding a two-iron low under the trees; he would rather be finding just the right words to explain a point than stopping a wedge a foot from the hole from a downhill lie in the trap; he would rather be reading a note of thanks from a student than knocking a seven-iron in the hole from 157 yards. His work has always been a game he could not master.

CHAPTER 12

The Critical Life

You wonder: What does it mean to live with a critical eye, an eye that's always assessing, always deciding questions of worth, always saying what's good or bad? What does it mean to judge others? What does it mean to say someone else does not measure up? By what right do you set certain standards? How can you not? What does it mean to judge yourself? By what right do you evaluate? What is at stake? To discover the heart of such questions, you track your day.

You wake up in the morning with a cat in your face. Aggravated by the purring and by a poor night's sleep, you feel your body's lack of readiness to begin the day. You note the difficulty you have swinging your legs out of bed and resent that you must use some effort to get up on your feet. You glance outside and you think that the day looks grim. You look at your wife, still sleeping, and wonder why the cat always decides to nudge you. Downstairs, you gently pat the other cat, who is asking for food. You open a can of chicken tuna for them and note the watery texture. You recognize that they have definite opinions about the matter. You go outside, find the paper, pleased at the delivery boy's careful placement. You fix yourself a cup of coffee, reheated from the day before. You taste its sourness. You begin to read. As you take in piece after piece, you assess—you're pleased that a referendum for a new school will be voted upon in the next election, you're unhappy with the increased allocations for the military, you're amused by a Dilbert cartoon, and so on.

After you finish the paper, you move into the bathroom. You brush your teeth, taking some pleasure in the taste of the toothpaste. You wash, and as you do so, you see yourself—you notice your face with its growing lines, your belly round as a watermelon, your hair flat as forgotten wet hay, your fingers stiff and swollen. You dress and discard a piece of lint from your shirt. You remove some cat hair from your pants. You notice that your favorite shoes are becoming worn. Your white, middle-class, middle-aged male body is ready for the day.

You call to your daughter to get out of bed. You know you will have to call several more times before she'll respond. This is a daily ritual. You call twice more. You fix your daughter a bowl of cereal with too much sugar. After seeing how good it looks, you fix a bowl for yourself, even though you usually don't eat anything in the morning. You are enjoying the cool crunchy taste when your daughter strolls in, wrapped in a blanket. You notice that part of the blanket is dragging on the floor but decide not to comment. "Good morning, darling," you say, reading her mood and speculating on the likelihood of her making the bus for school. You say as nicely as you can, "If you don't hurry, you'll miss the bus." "Don't worry," she responds, "I'll make it." Twenty minutes later you watch the bus go by without her. You are miffed.

Your wife comes down as you and your daughter are about to leave. You listen to her cheerful and loving good-bye to your daughter right after you have scolded her for her tardiness. You watch your daughter act as sweet as any child can be. You roll your eyes. In the car, you welcome the sound of your old 1985 Honda Civic starting right up. Your daughter begins working the radio buttons, seldom landing on a station that you would select. When she stumbles upon a song that you like, she, despite your protest, slides right over it. You turn the radio down and she turns it back up. You turn it down again and say, "If this isn't loud enough, it can go off." She rolls her eyes. You notice but say nothing. You hate starting the day this way with your daughter. After you drop her off at school, you tune in NPR. You hate starting your day at the office later than you anticipated.

At the office, you greet the staff and notice that the person you work most closely with looks tired, perhaps upset. You ask, "Is everything alright?" You hear a not-very-convincing "Everything's fine." You say, "Are you sure?" and after a second assurance, you suppress your suspicion and go about your business. But she stays in your mind. You worry that the man she has been living with is still not treating her right. You never liked him—his talk always seemed too loud, too dismissive of everyone, including her. You wonder if you should say anything to her about him but wisely decide that it would be presumptuous to do so.

In your own office, you look at your coffee mug and regret that you didn't wash it the day before. Coffee is a necessity, though, so you clean it. Pouring a cup, you enjoy the smell. You sip, not wanting to burn yourself, and then you read the messages you still have to answer, check your calendar for appointments and meetings, and make a list of what you must get done. You brace yourself for a long day.

You begin to grade a set of papers you've promised back to your students. The first paper you select begins with the sentence, "In my speach, I want to do a poem I always liked alot." You cringe, wondering how a student majoring in speech communication could misspell "speech," how in the second round of performances he could still call his presentation a speech, and how a junior in college could believe that that sentence would be an adequate opening to his essay. With all the authority of the academy behind you, you grade him down "alot." Before moving on to the next, you give his page-and-a-half essay a D without thinking about the racism, classism, and sexism of academic standards and without celebrating the fact that the student claims a deep affinity for a poem. The second paper is well written but says very little: B-. Next on the pile is an essay from your favorite student, the one who always seems so engaged with the material, so willing to participate in any discussion, so open to criticism. You know that even if her behavior is just an act, performance matters. She does not disappoint: A. You work through the batch, assigning grades, sometimes delightfully surprised and sometimes dismayed, sometimes conscious of what is guiding your judgments, sometimes not.

A colleague, bursting into your office, exclaims, "I'm so angry I don't know what to do. Read this review." He hands you several pages and then continues, "How could a reviewer read my piece that way? How could the editor agree with that reviewer? I'll bet he didn't even read the piece." You say, fearing that the editor and reviewer are probably right, "I'll be glad to read your essay, look these responses over, and tell you what I think." You have been just where he is. You remember the frustration of trying to please anonymous readers whose values seem as hidden as land mines. You remember the anger that arises from their cutting words, words that seem to say you are worthless. You remember the disappointment, pushing down on you, weighing on you, sinking into you. You believe you give them too much power in your life. As your colleague leaves, you wonder if he will place enough pieces in the right journals to get tenure. You glance at the pile of papers you just graded.

Your mind wanders. You think to yourself: My friend is caught; my students are caught; I'm caught. Everyone is caught in the same critical grind, giving out and taking in comments designed to say how we are positioned, rated, ranked. Even when you are situated on the top, you know that judgment carries a cost for those on the bottom. You think you could write an article that laments this fact. You imagine writing it in the second person, inviting identification. But then you worry that not everyone feels criticism's weight, that not everyone feels its never-ending presence. You ask yourself if you are just tired after years of pronouncements.

You pull yourself back from your speculations about the critical life. You have about thirty minutes before your first class, not the amount of time you like to have to prepare. You check the syllabus to see what you are supposed to cover. It's a familiar topic, one you have presented many times before. You jot down a few themes you want to cover, but you don't feel quite ready to face your students. In class, you pretend that you are ready; you note what you hope to accomplish. You mention a friend's research because you always found her way of framing the issues you are discussing particularly rich. The hour, to your relief and delight, goes well. At the end of class, you applaud your own effort, remembering that the classroom is your favorite place to be.

After your first class, a prospective graduate student calls inquiring about the status of his application into the program. Following a script you have used before, you answer, "I'm sorry to report that the graduate committee did not recommend that you be awarded a graduate teaching assistantship in our first round of offers. We have placed your name on an alternate list." Silence, and you sense the pain associated with your words. Other calls of inquiry come and responses to that same script vary:

"Fine. I just wanted to check before I accepted the offer from the University of Texas."

"Could you tell me why I was rated so low?"

"When do you think you might know if I'll make it in?"

Based upon their responses, you move some higher and some lower on the alternate list. Some you drop off the list altogether.

The calls you dread come from those you've decided you will not accept into the program. Your line is: "I'm sorry to say that the graduate committee did not feel that you were a good match for our program." You know what is coded in the word "match": We do not think you will do well in our program because what you want to study has nothing to do with what we offer (didn't you look at what we said we offer?), because everyone who wrote a letter of recommendation for your file indicated that you are not graduate-student material (didn't you realize that the people you asked for a recommendation would not write positively about you?), because given your prior academic record it seems unlikely that you will be successful in graduate school (didn't you think your 2.3 GPA and your bottom–ten-percent GRE scores would hurt your case?). You know your decision will have consequences in their lives. You know your decision will carry defining power. You know your decision hurts. You know, most of the time, what you are trying to perpetuate.

You understand that everything and everybody is judged in a market economy. Whether it is from the corporate executive's dictates, the academic's scrutiny, or a grandparent's gentle reminder, appraisal comes to all. Everything and everybody is given a price, an established worth. And you know that with every critical remark you make, you are participating in the commodification of everything and everybody. You are marking value, sticking on a price tag with each assessment, turning some things and some people into damaged goods. You see too how criticism itself is commodified as it colonizes social life. Your assessments, your glorifications and condemnations, become only something else to buy or discard, something else that moves people to the auction block. You do not see a way to escape criticism's ceaseless production. You do not want to let go of your standards.

Mail arrives. As you collect yours from your faculty box, you are pleased to see two journals, *Communication Monographs* and *Performing Arts Journal*; a book catalog from the University of Chicago Press promising discounts to 90 percent; and several first-class letters. You thumb through your *Communication Monographs*. You see five articles, most by more than one author, on topics of interest to you but located in a paradigmatic logic you find less than convincing. You read the abstracts and shake your head, not because you are confused by the content but because you cannot understand how the scientific model continues to thrive in the discipline given the number of arguments that show why the heart needs to accompany the head, particularly with such topics as communication apprehension, intimacy, compliance-gaining strategies, communication competence, gender, relational maintenance, and empathy. You place the issue on a stack of material you plan to read. During the next several months, you will keep skipping over it until you finally put it on your bookshelf alongside other unread *Monographs*.

You imagine the assessment the authors of the these articles might give your work: self-serving and self-indulgent, not generalizable, insufficiently grounded in current research, not appropriate as scholarly discourse, unacceptable method, superficial examination, no contribution to the accumulation of knowledge. You know the reasons for those readings, but you believe they miss the point. You write to create an evocative resonance, to call together a company of voices who feel the burden and pain of criticism's sting, to open a space for dialogue.

You pick up the *Performing Arts Journal* from your pile of mail. You see several pieces that you will read, pieces by the same group of contributing editors that appear over and over in the journal's pages, pieces that imply that performance only occurs in New York City. You resent this New York coterie that perpetuates their own interests but would never admit to such a thing. It would seem petty, small, provincial.

The University of Chicago Press catalog promises, you begin to see, 90 percent discounts only on titles you don't want. There are, however, several that intrigue: Marjorie Perloff's *Writing Poetry in the Age of Media*, Charles E. Reagan's *Paul Ricoeur: His Life and His Work*, and Patricia Fumerton's *Cultural Aesthetics: Renaissance Literature and the Practice of Social Ornament*. But the title that makes you take out your checkbook ($19.95 for paper) is Greg Dening's *Performances*. You read that Stephen Greenblatt believes Dening is the "most brilliant ethnohistorian writing today." You are anxious to see how Dening's study of time and place will use performance, whether it will lay claim to performance as a special activity or simply as a synonym for doing. As you write out your check, you speculate about why in this 47-page catalog there are no subject headings for communication, performance studies, or theatre. You consider how each of these fields struggles for academic legitimacy, how each makes birthright claims from their English father, how each resents its position.

Your first-class mail contains several pieces you are anxious to open. You quickly go through the letters that you know pertain to the graduate program. You open application materials—transcripts, late letters of recommendation, GRE scores, etc.—paperwork you will file later. You scan the materials quickly, noting what might be important. You receive one letter accepting and one rejecting your offer to do graduate work in your program. You mark their names, one with a "yes" and the other with a "no," thinking that if you had to lose one of these two people, you wish it had been the other one. Of your fifteen initial offers, twelve have accepted. You are pleased. You call an applicant from the alternate list, make the offer, and hear a sigh of relief. The applicant, now effusive, accepts immediately and you sense that you have called the right person.

Your mail also contains your self-addressed, stamped envelope from the *Georgetown Review*, a response to a group of poems you submitted several months before. You feel the weight of the envelope and guess that they haven't taken any of your poems. You open the envelope and find a standard rejection slip addressed to "Dear Contributor" and signed "The Editors." It reads, "Thank you for submitting your work to our magazine. Unfortunately, it doesn't meet our needs. We wish you luck in placing it elsewhere." You look for some indication that your poems were read, considered, perhaps a signature or a short comment on one of the poems. You find nothing. You wonder if you are wasting your time sending out your third-rate poems. Perhaps you should just save yourself the trouble, not to mention the postage.

You consider for a moment the difference you feel when some of your poems are rejected and when a scholarly essay of yours is turned down. For you, writing poems is your avocation, a necessary one that hangs on you like clothes. It helps keep confusion at bay, but it is not your job. Writing articles is; it is what you are supposed to know how to do. It is what you were trained to do. It is what you claim is essential to an academic life. So when one of your articles is rejected, when the reviewers point out the silliness of your ideas, when the editor doesn't even have an encouraging word, you feel as if you have been punched. Usually it takes you several days to get back up. Remembering this, you doubt that you gave your colleague the support he needed when he came in earlier complaining about his reviews.

You want to be the kind of person who offers judgments that humanize, that make us better people. You try, like feminists have taught you, to work with additive rather than corrective models. You often cast your comments within a contingent frame, noting the basis for your critical responses while indicating why other perspectives might call your claims into question. You study the situation to determine how you might speak with interpersonal sensitivity. Yet judgments, whether given or received, seem to move inside the body. First and foremost, criticism is always felt. You wonder how often its effect is simply to harden us.

Back to your mail. You received a note from a former student who wants several letters of recommendation. You will comply, but you are sorry that the person is not happy with her current placement. You had thought it was a good spot for her, and when you look at where she is applying, you doubt if she has found a better fit. You wonder what percentage of your colleagues believe that their department is a happy home for their work. As you put her letter aside, you notice that you haven't finished your coffee. You sip; it's cold and bitter. You look at your watch, wondering how long until lunch. You are surprised and sorry that most of the morning is gone.

You go to lunch with several colleagues, a daily ritual that can range from delightful to tiresome. As a result of the difficult faculty meeting from the day before, your and your colleagues' lunch talk is filled with cautious repairs. The faculty were split over who they should hire. The vote was 8 to 7, and no one left the two-hour meeting happy. You recognize how the split vote reflected different directions for the department. It cut to the core of departmental identity, each side dangerously implying who among those present had value. You found one faculty member's pronouncements particularly annoying. It seemed a shame that the debate had to take place over the bodies of the two candidates for the position. Over lunch you reaffirm a commitment to community and pledge never to buy French onion soup in that place again.

You rush back from lunch to make a 1:00 preliminary examination meeting. You sit in a room with two other colleagues and listen to a student attempt to justify why he is prepared to write an essay that would deconstruct acting theories. You doubt if he knows deconstruction or acting theories. You ask a simple question: "What acting theories do you want to address?" He mentions only Stanislavski and Brecht, and the more he talks, the more you are convinced that he cannot write a successful answer to a question on that theme. You engage in disappointing interaction on several other themes, and after he leaves the room so the committee can plan his questions, you feel sad and trapped. You know that he will not do well, no matter how much you tailor the questions to his strengths, no matter how long you will struggle to write a fair question that he might have a chance of answering, no matter whether or not you back off from your standards. You would like to run from it all, from all the words that pin down, for better and worse, person after person. But there is no place to run. Judgment permeates the academy. Judgment permeates home life. Judgment permeates the corporate world. Every day is judgment day.

By the time the meeting is over, you are late for your next class, Narrative Theatre. You start talking as you enter: "Let's get started. Sorry I'm late. Who's first?" The assignment—to write and perform a personal narrative—often generates the best work of the semester. The first performer tells a moving narrative about how easily her foot slid into her recently deceased mother's shoes as she was cleaning out her closet. During the critique, you applaud her use of the metaphor of stepping into her mother's shoes as well as the delicate and powerful restraint in the telling. You make it quite clear to the class that this was a performance you liked. Second, a tale of drinking, a "night to remember, (if I could), with an old friend." The rhetoric of the piece troubles you in its celebratory tone of drunken debauchery as a male bonding ritual. You are disturbed about how the audience laughs at this story and try reframing the performance from a comedy to a tragedy. Third, an African American student mocks white speech and middle-class values in her insightful and hilarious high school memory of white teachers telling her how she could "'Go places.' Talkin' like they knew what Jesse Jackson was all about, they would add, 'You could be somebody,' as if I wasn't anybody unless I went to college." Not wanting the class to miss the important message of this piece, you spend too much time discussing issues of class and race and forget to praise the performance. The final performance is disheartening—it's clear the student simply did not prepare. He assumes that the personal narrative form provides an opportunity to speak without rehearsal, without carefully choosing language, without craft. You suggest that the piece is going in good directions and that with work, it could be quite effective. The critique, though, is just a way to hide your anger at the student's lack of effort. As you leave the classroom, you are satisfied with your responses to the performances. They are, of course, predictable.

Returning to your office, you encounter a graduate student whose dissertation defense is scheduled for the next day. You read the dissertation over the weekend and, although it was not particularly ambitious or exciting, it seemed acceptable. You say, feeling that you are too close to a lie to make you completely comfortable, "I'm looking forward to tomorrow's meeting. I think you have a good study." You see the relief. Knowing that you are willing to sign off, you are glad to see the student, a student you truly like, let some anxiety drop away.

Checking for messages in the main office, you hear a colleague ask, "How is that piece on criticizing everything coming?" "It's coming," you answer, somewhat embarrassed that you haven't yet finished such a short piece. "I'd love to read it when you're done." "Sure," you say, thinking that the piece feels too fragile at this point to be placed in that colleague's hands. You want to protect it, to keep it safe, to sustain your faith in it. You do not want a public viewing until you feel strong. In your office, you click on the "The Critical Life" icon. It's been several weeks since you last looked at the piece. You begin to read: You find a typo and fix it; you change a word because it was used just a sentence before; you decide a paragraph isn't working and place in brackets "Ugh" as an indicator to rework. The piece seems distant, difficult to recover, suspect. You cannot enter its spirit, its depressing weight. You cannot regain your belief in it. You know what good scholarship is. You are, after all, a reviewer for several journals, and you doubt if this piece measures up. Discouraged but unwilling to abandon the project, you hit "save" and click off.

You are off to a 4:00 College of Liberal Arts Council meeting. On the agenda is whether the doctoral program in history should be eliminated. You feel torn. You know that the history department is not one of the stronger programs on campus—it doesn't fare well on productivity and quality measures—and that the university cannot continue to support its full complement of graduate programs, but you resent having to vote against colleagues who stand before you pleading their case, and you resent being used by the administration when it suits their purposes. Following a tense debate, you vote to maintain the program for the second year in a row, but you don't feel good about your decision. History is saved. You leave the meeting more than ready to be home.

The radio is still set on NPR. You begin listening to the top news stories, but your mind returns to your day at work. You think of passing comments that you made and consider whether you said the right thing at the right time. You remember comments made to you and wonder how you should understand what was said. The one remark that lingers with you is when a colleague said, "Jeff likes your class." Although seemingly complimentary, the remark carried a tone of condescension, an obligatory pat, perhaps even a touch of surprise. It didn't feel good. What made it worse is that you think your colleague was implying that Jeff had said much more, more than he should share. It galled you that Jeff, a mediocre student at best, was talking to this colleague about the quality of your teaching. The whole encounter felt like a power play. NPR pulls you from these thoughts with a witty commentary on the trouble a woman encounters when trying to buy a car if she is accompanied by a man.

Pulling in the drive, you see several bikes arranged on the lawn like grazing cows. You know that the cowboys, visiting your daughter, are inside. You cringe and hope they haven't eaten all the grub or destroyed the ranch. To your surprise, they—seven of them, four boys if you are counting correctly—are watching a movie and nibbling on popcorn. Some you recognize, some you don't. Their heads turn as you enter and your daughter barely musters, "Oh, hi." You return the greeting and watch their heads swing back to the television. Your daughter reports, "Mom is still at work. She won't be home until later." You nod and then plop down in the study, your favorite room. You look at your bookshelves with pleasure and then guilt, thinking of all the titles you haven't had a chance to read. You pick up a journal but decide that you're too tired even to be an adequate reader. You resent that there is never enough time, never enough hours that aren't scheduled, never enough free space. Before you know it, you are dozing and you startle yourself awake by the weight of your head dropping. You rub the drool from the side of your mouth. Your ten-minute nap makes you feel worse. You rub your stiff neck and curse the fact that departmental politics kept you awake much of last night.

You decide to fix yourself two peanut-butter sandwiches before your 7:00 rehearsal. The bread is stale. You choke them down with some milk and leave a twenty for your daughter and her friend, the one still remaining in the house, to order a pizza. Her friend is one you have always liked—friendly, at ease with adults, always ready with a smile. Your daughter thinks she is a suck-up but most of the time enjoys her company. You approve of this friend and feel comfortable leaving for rehearsal after making sure they have ordered the pizza.

NPR news is over. You slip in your *Les Miserables* tape. It plays "One Day More" and you sing along with volume, with passion, with a voice that your mother insisted that you reserve for those times when you are not in public. You are delighted by the squirrel that crosses in front of your car after you stopped for a light as if it knew the green/red code. You are annoyed by the driver who honks to pass you while you are going ten miles over the speed limit. "What an ass!" you say to yourself. As you pull in the parking lot for the the-atre, you notice the sun sliding from the sky. You stop to take in the pink colors, soft and seductive as cotton sheets.

You are scheduled to work the first three scenes of a play you and your cast created through improvisation. The play seems promising. Eager to see it on its feet, you look forward to getting it blocked. You love helping actors find just the right action to punctuate a moment. You love seeing bodies take space, claim it, give it meaning. You love, when it's working, the seemingly natural flow of bod-ies responding to bodies, moving here and there, as if set into motion by some magical hand. Always, you try to negotiate the space between the actors' and your own desires. You never want to become a puppet-master. Working with this expe-rienced cast, you are quick to back off from suggestions they find suspicious or uncomfortable. They have earned your trust. You have watched them take even your most inane ideas and make them work. You feel fortunate to have this cast;

challenged; and, at times, useless. You are not sure if you have earned *their* trust. By the end of rehearsal you are convinced, even though you only got through the first two scenes, that you are off to a solid start. The play is working, the action is working, the characters are working. You leave feeling content.

The night is settling in. When you arrive home, the house is dark except for a small light in your daughter's room. You're pleased that the living room is back in order—no pizza box with half a pizza left over, no dirty glasses and napkins, no large bowls with popcorn kernels settled on the bottom, no pop cans left around. In the living room, your cats, curled together and sleeping in the middle of your favorite chair, don't bother to lift their heads when you enter. You go to your daughter's room. You want the final interaction of the day with your daughter to be positive, particularly on a day when you have had so little contact. You go to her room, sit on the side of her bed, and ask, "How was your day?" "Fine," she answers, still more interested in the television than speaking with you. But after a moment, she turns the television off and looks at you: "Mom was exhausted so she went to bed." You begin chatting, sharing this and that, talking in the quiet tones of late night. Such moments are gifts, given without thought, given like gravy. Nourished, you tell your daughter to get some sleep. You quickly slip out of your clothes and into bed, trying not to wake your wife. She mumbles from her sleep, "Sorry I had to go to bed. How are you?" "Fine," you answer, "Go back to sleep." You snuggle enjoying the comfort of another body next to yours.

You drift off thinking that no moment passes without a critical eye. No moment escapes. Your day is nothing more than a series of pleasures and dis-pleasures, a series of stances, object lessons in attitude. You are right; you are wrong. You are gracious; you are cruel. You are a critic. You are who you are because you exist in a critical life. You have no choice. You speak from your white, middle-class, middle-aged male body. You speak from the academy, per-petuating its logic, its standards, perpetuating the system. You speak from your vested interests. You speak out of belief.

Having tracked your day, you examine what you have done. You sense that you have a better feel for what is at stake in the ongoing critical process. You say to yourself: It isn't about demonstrating critical faculties, showing critical superiority, or even striving to become better; it is about how people feel liv-ing under its power. You will read each passage of your essay—some you will like and some you won't. You will do some editing, changing a sentence here, a word there, dropping a paragraph that you think is too disclosive. You will be open to criticism. You will revise to get at the heart of the matter. You will think the piece is better than it is. You will wonder how you will be read: too detached? too cynical? too sentimental? You will continue to evaluate it. You will continue to evaluate yourself. And when all is said and done, you will know that you are not critical. Others can and will take your place.

CHAPTER 13

Playing the Field

co-authored with Elyse Pineau

Epilogue

To begin with an epilogue is to say that experience is prologue to explanation. It is to allow oneself the luxury of privileging the living moment, the situated individual who is constantly in the ongoing process of constructing meaning. It is to recognize that the life of a community exceeds, in its richness and complexity, the sense-making activity of any one of its participants. It is to claim that an imaginative evocation of voices from that community life, spoken from within the heart of the playing field, yields as compelling an explanation of culture as any distanced description offered from the sidelines. It is to insist that all members of a community are contributing members of a cultural team, that all members are players worth watching. And it is to trust that explanation may find its fullest articulation in the literary.

We are two actors in a scholarly community, performing in an organizational culture that has many spectators, commentators, and critics. We hear the ever-present chatter from within. We struggle to make sense of what we hear, to understand the rules that govern our actions, the play-by-play strategies that guide our movements, and the titles that mark our successes. We seek a language we can trust, one that catches the experience. We gain authenticity by virtue of our location within the organization; we resist any claim to representative authority on the same basis. We seek a new press. We believe, following H. L. Goodall and many others, that the "mysteries" of organizational life are essentially poetic; they often elude categorization, defy definition, and evaporate under the cold scrutinizing gaze of traditional scholarly discourse. To revel in the mysteries of the academic game, we search for the evocative. We embrace the poetic to discover a truth, to present a reality of living and working within the academy.

Learning Which Way to Run

How to cover the bases? Assume everyone can play. Believe that the rules could change. Trust that dialogue has worth. Let there be voices. Let those who can be heard begin the game, open the field. Let us cheer the start of a new season.

Such an idea is a player's folly. But begin anyway.

I tried to look it up in the Rulebook but someone must have misplaced that chapter. I tried to ask the old-timers, but they told me that having to ask meant I was already falling behind. I tried to listen, but no one ever spoke about it. I tried to watch, but they all made it seem so invisible. I knew it was there. I just couldn't put my finger on what "it" was.

Someone is always in, someone out. Learn to speak the talk, learn to smile when needed, learn to quote those on top. With some, you can't go wrong. Some you pretend to know, some you pretend to read, some you pretend to believe. When you're in the know, you know.

Wait. Not fair. Surely some play for real, some make it count.

Some do it better than others. Some have a knack for it. Everything depends on how you play.

Surely this couldn't be it.

On Being a Rookie

Standing in the halls of your first convention, you cannot imagine why everyone is rushing. You connect a face with a name and are surprised that the person looks, well, quite like everyone else. You eat alone, watch a little television, and go to sleep. You have selected five programs you want to attend tomorrow. At the second session, you meet someone who seems as lost as you. It is calming to talk with someone; it is the simple pleasure of sharing impressions. Tomorrow you will give your first presentation. You have rehearsed, even more than you planned. You don't remember much except faces. A few people say nice things. You are pleased but not sure what to trust. You will return one vitae line and one friend richer. Next year you will rush off to meet her.

There is a fine line between idealism and naiveté, passion and arrogance, creativity and thin ice, between espousing the idea of dialogue and engaging in it publicly, between advocating alternative styles of discourse and daring to enact one before your peers. Part of being a rookie means not always knowing which side of the line you are standing on. It also means that missteps are forgiven.

Perhaps.

Hanging with the "Boys"

Steps toward becoming a member of the team:

1. *You see who is going to dinner with whom. You watch.*
2. *You decide you want to go. You wait your turn.*
3. *You go. You learn the rules. You figure out what it takes to play well.*
4. *You laugh freely around the table, deep rich laughs that claim the space as yours.*

Whose is the biggest? Be careful how you put it on the table. It is an ugly game.

Claim the space as mine? And what space would that be? I'm not a boy. I don't hang. And tables are for eating.

Care to become a member of my team?

1. You invite your friends to dinner. We share the cab.
2. We order the family combo, taking turns tasting each others' dishes.
3. We shake off the rules. Just playing is good enough.
4. We laugh freely around the table. Deep, rich laughs that open up the space that's ours.

Whose is the biggest? What a stupid question.

To hang does not require anatomy.

Umpires, Referees, and Other Legislators

There are umpires, referees, and legislators in this game. They write the rules, set all the markers. They stand in the middle of the field watching the boundaries. Often they tell you how well they can play. Some are insecure "has-beens" from another time, always looking over their shoulders. Some are sure they have it right. Their time will come.

Insiders believe they can write your article better than you can. They enjoy telling you this at regular intervals. Outsiders do not understand what you have written. They also enjoy telling you this. You listen. Sometimes it is very helpful. You do not enjoy it.

Spectators and Hecklers

This is a game, like most, of watching and being watched.

You feel their gaze heavy on you as you take your mark. You gauge the distance, test the wind, take a firm grip.

Thumbs up, thumbs down.

The crowd freezes you with their stare. What do you expect to read in their faces?

You make the call.

Heroes and Role Models

You know who they are. Their mere entrance onto the playing field can sweep an audience to its feet. Their names on the roster sell tickets, pack the stands. Their autograph graces book jackets, journals, recommendations. We line our bookshelves with mementos of their careers. Their endorsement attracts consumers, ensures program success. Every young hotshot wants a crack at breaking their record. Once elected to the Hall of Fame, they move into management, coaching, and commentary. Eventually, their numbers are retired and they pass away into legend. We are a nostalgic people.

Students of the Game

They want to play so badly. You tell them to wait their turn, to learn the ropes, that their time will come. You give them what you got. You show them your best pitch. But you know that some will never make it.

Clichés for the uninitiated:

> *"You've got to really want it."*
> *"You've got to keep reading."*
> *"You've got to love the classroom."*
> *"You've got to network with your colleagues."*
> *"You've got to write every day."*
> *"You've got to publish."*
> *"You've got to publish."*
> *"You've got to publish."*
> *"You've got to publish."*
> *"You've got to publish."*
> *"You've got to publish."*
> *"You've got to publish."*

Seven pieces should do it. Seven of the right kind, in the right places.

What all-important border did I cross to become one of "us" instead of one of "them?" Do they know that it doesn't get any easier? The hours are just as long, the papers more complex, the critiques more cutting.

Seven pieces? And would you count this piece?

Coaches, Mentors, and Bosses

"I can take you where you want to go."
  How do I know I want to go there?
"Trust me."
  Well, I'm here.
"That's not where I meant."
  It doesn't matter. It's where I am.

I was a kid, golf club in one hand and a beer in the other. "Come on, boy, put those down. You've got what it takes," he said. I gave them up.
  "Listen," she said, "listen." I did.
  "Relax, go play some golf, have a beer," he said.

Feeling the Pressure

The pressure of the top is displaying the right to be there. The pressure of the bottom is displaying the right to not be there. The pressure of the middle is displaying which way you want to go.

You're only as good as your last season.

Making the Team

They approve me. They approve me not. They approve me. . . . Going up for tenure signifies that you've paid your dues, moved through the ranks, documented consecutive successful seasons, impressed management with your earned-run average, fostered team morale, become a role model, inspired a fan club, made the final cut. Sometimes it just feels like you're out in left field plucking petals.

The Grand Slam, the Slam Dunk

It is in their eyes when they call your name. You know you matter at least at this point in time, at this moment, for one person. You allow yourself to believe the fictions you teach. You may, of course, be fooling yourself.

I believe those fictions. Foolish me.

Your most promising program is scheduled for 9:00 on Saturday night. Dropping your most significant paragraph, your article appears. Your book comes out with a misspelling on the binding.

Still, your name is on the program, the article has appeared, and the book is in print.

You are named to an important position. It's a clerk's job.

But they knew your name.

Free Agent

Before becoming a free agent, you should answer all of the following questions positively:

1. Do you have impressive stats?
2. Are you a team leader?
3. Can you play all positions with equal skill?
4. Is there a need for your talent?
5. Are you a dispensable commodity?

> *Who will make the team? Who goes to the majors? Who goes to the minors? Who gets the highest bid? Who do you want around? Who do you need to win the College Bowl?*

Box scores don't lie.

Ticket Prices

> *It will cost you to get in.*

How do you reckon the cost?

> *And, of course, the cost is much more than money. Give us your time.*

In evenings and weekends lost to the computer? Vacations squeezed between convention panels?

> *Give us your mind.*

The luxury of time spent on ideas rather than basic survival? The privilege of thinking, reading, speaking, writing, performing?

> *Give us your family. Give us your life.*

Life decisions on hold until tenure?

> *Now, let's see, have you given enough?*

You get what you pay for.

> *You can sit in the bleachers but you really can't see the whole game from there.*

With this game, it's enough to just break even.

Hearing the Fat Lady Sing

You know you're at the end of your career when:

> *no one wants to hear about your plays that have always worked*
> *everyone knows exactly what play you'll call next*
> *your yellowed playbook crumbles like clichés*
> *you can't even put your playbook on the latest equipment*
> *your plays have become part of the history of the game*
> *you think you can get away with using "Hearing the Fat Lady Sing"*
>   *as a subheading*

It's Only a Game

> *As a young boy, I would punch holes in my wall when I didn't win. My mother thought this was quite serious, not only for the wall but for me. She believed it was an index of my psychic health. I thought it was a perfectly reasonable response to not performing up to expectations.*

Early morning on the first day of the conference. Your paper is on social movements and political resistance. Anxiety. Last-minute rewrite. Scribbled outline. More anxiety. The headline reads: "Student Activists Massacred in Tiananmen Square." Silence. . . . You present your paper to polite applause.

> *Older now, I'm not sure what it means to win or lose. The rules of the game are less clear. As this game ends, who else wants to play? Good. Now where are boundaries? Who plays first?*

CHAPTER 14

Making Lists: Life at the University

On Teaching an Introduction to Graduate Studies Course

Today I told them that to be in the academy meant that they would always be behind, never able to read everything that they should, never able to even keep up with the new books in their specializations, never able to stop working.

Today I told them of the pure excitement I feel when I am browsing in a bookstore and I stumble across a title in my area of interest that I did not know existed. I take it from the shelf as carefully as one might reach for a newborn in a crib. I cradle it and run my finger down its spine. I love the smell, the freshness, the promise. I will not have the time I want to spend with it.

Today I told them that no matter how skilled they become, reviewers and editors will find something problematic in every single thing they will write. "Revise and resubmit" is cause for celebration.

Today I told them that finding the exact word, crafting the elegant sentence, and constructing the intricate paragraph is a pleasure unlike any other. Such pleasure comes from a struggle against confusion; it comes from a commitment to hope; it comes from a belief in the possible. Writing collides with and cripples cynicism.

Today I told them that unless they feel stupid during their graduate work, the faculty members are not doing their jobs. The Ph.D. is designed, I went on, to teach future scholars how little they know.

Today I told them that as a community of scholars, they will cut their critical teeth outside the classroom, in interaction with one another, in the pleasures of finding voice, of learning to say what they believe and believing what they say. Out of such efforts, they will make lifelong friends.

Today I told them that decisions about curriculum, about academic growth and survival, about educational vision have very little to do with the power or sophistication of academic arguments but instead are the product of how personalities bump against one another. People form allegiances and alliances. Some people are given credibility and some are not; some people are liked and some are not. Interpersonal relationships determine educational mission.

Today I told them that never will their own capacities be more challenged and their beliefs more evident than when they are given an opportunity to shape a program. Never will they be in a position to shape more lives.

Today I told them that even some community colleges are demanding that their faculty publish, despite insisting that their faculty carry a teaching load of fifteen to twenty-one hours per semester. Even adjunct faculty, faculty with no job security, no benefits, no office or support services, are expected to turn out the pages.

Today I told them that white pages seduce, pull you in, until you fill them with your own desire. Stare at that whiteness long enough and you will find what you have to say.

Today I told them that the vision of the academy as an ivory tower is being replaced with the notion of the academy as an industrial park—out with contemplation, in with mechanization.

Today I told them that more and more people from the business community are looking for college graduates who are trained in the liberal arts. We can train people to do specific tasks, they say, but we can't train them how to think.

Today I told them that if they want to have a happy career in the academy, never say anything against a colleague. I also said that it is almost impossible to follow that advice.

Today I told them how touched I was that a student acknowledged my help with her recent publication and how, even after many years, I am still embarrassed that I did not know enough to thank in print Dr. Joanna Maclay, who made my first publication possible. The academy, despite considerable evidence to the contrary, is capable of kindness.

Today I told them that unless they love teaching, there is no reason for them to stay in higher education. By the way, I added, most of your time will be taken by other tasks.

Today I told them, while some of them were fiddling with their pencils and some of them were preparing to take notes, "Thank you for letting me be here with you." I was sitting at the head of the table.

Today I told them that their field enjoys little respect within the academy. After all, it isn't counted among the sciences and it brings in few research dollars.

Today I told them that my bookshelves are lined with books of scholars in the field, a claim I could not have made just a few years ago since it has only been recently that we have contributed scholarly texts to the academic arena, texts whose authors are speaking not to undergraduate students but to other scholars.

Today I told them that more and more students see themselves as consumers and see teachers as merely the clerks who are hired to serve them. Class attendance can no more be expected than one can demand that customers come into a store. Grades are designed not to assess work but to satisfy the customers. Lecturing is considered problematic, not because it is considered intellectually bankrupt but because it is considered a poor marketing strategy.

Today I told them that maybe the economic metaphor used to conceptualize teacher-student relationships is less frightening if we think of students as clients who are seeking counsel. Maybe, I went on, conceptualizing the teacher-student relationships in any economic metaphor is poor pedagogy. Maybe the best teachers are those who, regardless of the cost-reward ratio, care about their students. Over and over again, those are the individuals who are named outstanding teachers.

Today I told them that the classes that get to be taught are those that fit the arbitrary 5-10-15 enrollment guidelines for economic efficiency. Any argument based in sound pedagogy and against such an arbitrary standard will not be heard.

Today I told them that what got me in the field was a teacher, Dr. Leland Roloff, who saw potential in a poor student, me, in his crowded classroom.

Today I told them that most universities say they evaluate their faculty on three criteria: teaching, research, and service. However, if a faculty member is a good colleague (i.e., collegial), then his/her colleagues will find ways, even when there is little to work with, to build the faculty member's case. If a faculty member is not a good colleague (i.e., collegial), his/her record of teaching, research, and service will matter very little.

Today I told them that the greatest compliment they could receive at the end of their careers would be if the faculty voted to replace them in kind.

Today I told them that by the time many of their colleagues receive tenure, they are so cynical that they retire on the job. It won't be long, I speculated, before tenure will become only a topic in a History of Higher Education course, if indeed that course has sufficient enrollment.

Today I told them of a colleague who managed to barely meet the minimal requirements for tenure but once tenured, flourished, producing article after article, book after book. When I asked my colleague to explain this, she said, "It is easier to work when you're not being watched."

Today I told them that their discipline is facing an identity crisis, that it lives in a constant state of paranoia (perhaps justified), and that few within the academy would insist that their department must be a part of a comprehensive university's offerings.

Today I told them that through the basic course, their discipline reaches most students who enter college. That, more than anything else, says that they matter.

Today I told them that I never heard of anyone not receiving tenure because of a poor service record.

Today I told them that service doesn't just mean committee work for their department, university, or professional organizations, nor does it just mean having an active presence in the community; it can also mean being of service to those they study.

Today I told them that their job is not to mediate faculty disputes; faculty share histories that students cannot and should not know. Faculty members, I argued, stay together for many years, often debating issues that cut to the core of their identities. Little wonder that tensions can run high.

Today I told them that the faculty will, more often than not, put their students' interests first. They will go to great lengths to protect them, to code suggestions without condemning their colleagues. Listen between the lines, I advised, to the counsel of your advisors.

Today I told them that they had to learn both the MLA and APA guidelines and that there are good reasons why changes are made with each edition. I just didn't always know what those good reasons were. I said that I was particularly fond of APA's 4th edition decision to indent author names so that authors not only don't have first names but are also more hidden than ever before. I was speaking, of course, as a writer.

Today I told them that such familiar metaphors as giving birth and initiation rite for writing a dissertation are apt. They would be wise, I added, not to offend their birth attendant or their tribal chief.

Today I told them that a dissertation can have defining power in a person's career, but it is not a career.

Today I told them that often citation is a tribute, an ethical act of honoring a colleague. Quoting may help build a case, but it is also a public act of giving applause.

Today I told them that their department survival often rests upon the whims of a dean, an academic vice-president, or a president who believes that administrators earn their keep by shaking things up. Beware, most of all, a dean, an academic vice-president, or a president from your own discipline who wants to help your department. Such people often do the greatest damage to your program.

Today I told them that the best administrators can easily be spotted by whether they take their primary audience to be higher or lower on the organizational chart. While they are looking up, no telling what or who they might step on.

Today I told them that if they want to publish, they need to be tough skinned since the reviews they will receive will often be brutal, will miss the intent of their essays, and will imply that they should not be in higher education after all. Knowing this, most faculty retreat to their office and close the door before reading their reviews.

Today I told them that to see their name in print, to read each of its letters across the top of a page, or to rub a finger over its imprint on the cover of a book satisfies deeply. It is a satisfaction that goes straight to the ego. It is one way the academy says you still can earn an A.

Today I told them that even after they publish their work, no one will ever say anything about it; it falls into an academic void until maybe one day you'll pick up a journal and see yourself quoted—not to prove an argument but to justify why more work needs to be done.

Today I told them that some days you will wonder why you are doing all this.

Today I told them that to publish is to be a part of disciplinary history. I told them that to teach is to change lives. I told them that to serve is to answer a calling. I hoped I wasn't depressing them with all this talk about life in the academy. I told them that there is no place I'd rather be.

They just looked at me, thinking about themselves.

Assessment and Other Strange Abnormalities

Let's create accreditation agencies that have the power to say we have no value. We'll live in such fear of those agencies we create that we'll spend an incredible number of faculty hours devoted to defending ourselves against them.

Let's publish textbooks, colorful ones full of pictures, pie charts, and big print with simple sentences so that we can train our students to be as dumb as we envision them when we write. Let's produce a new edition every two or three years so that we as well as our publishers can make a good profit off our students.

Let's set awards for teaching and try, year after year, to convince ourselves that teaching is valued as much as research in the academy. Let's persuade ourselves that we can measure good teaching by asking our students and each other to write in our own behalf.

Let's give our biggest salaries to those who are the most removed from our students. Then let's have them make all the important decisions about our students' educational needs.

Let's ensure that the activity we spend the most time with, grading, cannot be used as an assessment measure. Instead, let's get the faculty to establish objective criteria and measurement instruments that fulfill the requirements of the assessment office but that few faculty members see as valid.

Let's establish a Board of Directors to govern our university, making sure that all the appointments to the board are political appointees and that none has any academic credentials.

Let's form a union so that we can think of ourselves as automobile or garment workers who toil on the assembly line, so that we can compile merit grids for assessing all faculty, so that we can add another level of bureaucracy to the never-ending discussion of shared governance, so that we can ensure that we will have an adversarial relationship with the administration we claim we should have the right to hire.

Let's add committees, lots and lots of them, to find solutions to problems that administrators already know how they want to solve.

Let's teach more and more of our classes on the Web so that we can have less and less face-to-face contact with our students. Let's call it distance learning and claim that we are providing access to those who cannot reside on or commute to campus, despite the fact that most people who take the courses have access and despite the fact that while most see this as a sound marketing strategy, few believe that it is sound pedagogy.

Let's lower admission standards and then wonder why our retention rate has dropped. Then, to correct the retention problem, let's reduce what we require of our students so that more students will continue to pay tuition and after they graduate (knowing nothing) will give generously to the university that coddled them.

Let's fill our university bookstore with mugs, sweatshirts, and greeting cards. Let's keep only required books on the shelves so that students will think that reading is something they should do only when it is assigned.

Let's judge the worth of a university by the quality of its football team. Let's set up a system where the public cares much more about what the coach has to say than any faculty member. Let's pay the coach more than any other employee at the university and supplement his income with his own television show. Meanwhile, let's have student athletes labor for their tuition dollars while universities make millions off of their talents.

Let's design our universities with limited parking so that visitors, students, staff, and faculty will have such difficulty finding a place to park that they will just turn around and go home.

Let's insist that when the bell rings, we will send our students on their way regardless of what might be happening in the classroom. Let's demand that all our classes follow the same time schedule, regardless of content. Let's never let education interfere with efficiency.

Let's see how many people we can make who look just like us. Let's perpetuate our own kind.

Let's have the Faculty Senate decide during tight budgetary times which programs should stay and which programs should be cut. Let's call that shared governance and assume we are building a cooperative, interdisciplinary, educational environment for our students.

Let's decide that four years is just the right amount of time to teach all subjects to all students.

Let's generate reports, lots of them—self-studies, comparisons to peer universities, rankings, findings of internal and external review teams, graphs of this and that, long-range plans and short-term plans, mission statements—that nobody will read except when they are looking for some rationale for doing what they have already planned to do.

Let's allow one or two faculty members to create such a hostile departmental environment with their complaints, their grievances, and their untruths that the rest of the faculty stays away from the department as much as possible. Let's give the complaining, grieving, and lying faculty members more departmental resources in the hope that they will finally be satisfied. When they are not, let's be thankful that their faculty rights are being protected.

Let's hire a president, preferably male, who has no experience in education but who we claim is qualified because he has been running a major corporation or has held political office.

Let's force students to pay student fees that will permit entry into all the campus sporting events but none of the campus theatre productions, music concerts, dance recitals, film series, or art shows. Let's believe that we aren't teaching them what we value.

Let's, when determining who we should hire in a faculty line, reduce the complexity of the decision to undergraduate enrollment. Let's only count the number of bodies in each major. Let's simply forget about such things as differences in mode of instruction, program development, the mission of the department or the university, and especially, vision.

Let's take out insurance policies to protect ourselves from our students and from each other. Let's never change what we stated we would do on the syllabus because someone might sue. Let's make sure that whatever we do matches what the university catalogue says we will do.

Let's grade students higher and higher every semester, not because they are better than previous students but because we don't want the hassle of their complaints and because we can't afford to lose their tuition dollars.

Let's promise our students in all our promotional materials a piece of the American pie when they graduate. Let's show them graphs of how much more money they will make if only they are college graduates. Let's recruit them by hanging dollar signs in front of their faces. Then let's complain that our students are too focused on their careers.

Let's go to conferences to present our papers without bothering to attend any program but our own. Let's say we are going to the conferences for professional development.

Let's isolate departments and pit one against another for limited resources. Let's watch how they close themselves off from the rest of the university. Let's notice how they live in fear, afraid they will be attacked, afraid that all their hard work will be lost when another of their kind begins to package and teach what they have or when a dean, thinking he/she knows just what the university needs, acts on a hunch.

Let's write job descriptions that lock us into decisions we don't want to make.

Let's never touch a student because showing affection might be misconstrued as sexual harassment. Let's never close our office door when a student wants to discuss a problem because you never know when you are being set up.

Let's generate theory after theory but never test any of them in the communities where we live.

Let's hire outside consultants to do what our faculty have the expertise to do. Then, after paying the consultants, let's regret that we don't have the funds to do what they recommended.

Let's tell our students, who we believe should be capable of dealing with most sophisticated ideas of thinkers throughout recorded time, that they have to live in approved housing.

Let's fashion a budgeting system that punishes programs for not spending every penny they were given by cutting their budget the following year. Let's keep the budget tied to a yearly cycle so that at the end of every year, everyone will try to spend what they were given, regardless of what they might need.

Let's vote to tenure faculty members we don't think should be tenured because if we don't, we'll lose the line.

Let's establish remedial programs on campus to accomplish what the high schools failed to teach. Let's say that the students who are enrolled have great potential as long as they are paying tuition.

Let's assume that being professional means being right instead of being collegial. Let's call each other colleagues as we treat each other as fools.

Let's devise a university we can sell like Nike shoes, built on the back of cheap labor, designed for profit, and filled with lies. We'll just do it.

Teachers

Leland H. Roloff

Maybe it was his voice, deep and bold, coming, it always seemed to me, from the earth's core, smoldering, hot, driving up and up and until it found just the place it wanted to erupt, just the moment it wanted to command, just the audience it wanted to reach. It came to gather me in, to surround me, to swallow me whole, and it took me away. I hung onto every syllable, to every pause, to every inflection. He came to me as Apollo and Dionysus, complete.

Maybe it was his stature, so erect, so straight, elevated beyond all doubt. He always seemed taller than my 6'3" frame but wasn't. He always seemed above us all, looking down like a benevolent god. He always seemed present.

Maybe it was his deep eyes, how they seemed so focused that his brows folded in just to be part of it all.

Maybe it was that slight tilt of his head to his right side, his slight rocking, as if he were cocked, ready to spring into his point, ready to be unleashed. Maybe it was that he never let go of it all. Maybe it was always the promise of what was to come.

Maybe it was the time he exclaimed to something I said, "Yes, yes, yes." His enthusiastic outburst was so shocking to me that I lost forever what little insight I might have had.

Maybe it was his provocative curiosity. He flew through the world like a gliding hawk, circling above, diving for what others could never see in order to feed the young. He could claw apart anything he found.

Maybe it was the first time I saw him find insight in a student's work that I was too simple to see. I listened to him make the case, a case that was beyond me but one that I sensed was right. I knew then, as I know now, that I needed to listen.

Maybe it was his intellectual prowess, how he could push ideas around with such ease and with such seriousness that you thought all ideas were his own.

Maybe it was his compassion. This Promethean figure, this bringer of fire, knew no bounds.

Joanna Maclay[1]

Having had Flannery O'Connor put in my bones, I wanted to line up all the academics I could think of. At back of the line would be the stupid and arrogant ones who thought they had all the answers, and then would come those who never tried to get any answers, and just ahead of them would be those who thought they had some answers but were often wrong, and then those who thought they had some answers and were often right but weren't arrogant about it, and then. . . . It was about this time I got really confused because I knew that Joanna was at the head of the line but that she was so far ahead that it wasn't really a line anyway and about that time a student came in waving a paper I had graded in my face and said, "You ain't nothing but a wart hog from the University of Illinois."

I wanted to come out, dressed in spiked heels and smoking a corncob pipe, but I know everyone would just say, "It takes all kind to make the world go 'round."

I wanted to say "Reach in your purse and git yourself a cigarette without no powder in it if you kin, Mrs. Maclay, 'cause I know you don't like no perfume cigarettes and 'cause I was hoping we could just have a nice long chat."

I wanted to perform Hazel Motes with such skill and passion that the Holy Spirit would just have to take notice, but I can hear Joanna saying, "You may be from the South, hon, but you sure don't have *Wise Blood*."

I wanted to say it was something I didn't want to do. It is something I ain't got no business doing. I stopped in front of the theatre where there was a large blond woman stuffing students into a classroom. I ain't going in no classroom like that, I said. I'm going home. I ain't going to wait around no classroom, I said, giving it a nervous look. I found myself moving down a row of chairs. Well, I ain't going to listen to her. I only like theatres that's got lots of singing in it. I ain't going to look at her. The first performance was about this woman who was getting along fine when she really wasn't. I drew my hat down and pulled my knees up in front of my face. The second performance was about a hairdresser who thought about all the things she could do with a petrified man. When I recovered myself, I was sitting against a theatre building and not thinking anymore about escaping my duty. I felt that the knowledge I couldn't avoid was almost on me.

I wanted to share the first draft of my prospectus, covered with red markings, covered with insight. Like Hulga with Manley Pointer, I don't want any lies between us: Joanna is an intellectual.

I wanted to remind you of how Joanna can read a few paragraphs from a short story and make you see things you never imagined were there. But, like a revelation, they are there.

I wanted to tell you that I went into the academic hayloft with Joanna and I said, "You ain't said you love me none." Well, to make a long story short, she showed me where my head joins on. I got me all kinds of good stuff like that.

I wanted to say that Joanna is bigger on the speech communication side than she is on the theatre side, but that would be a deliberate calculated falsehood. She's the same.

I wanted to show you Pelias's back, but it would be just a bunch of Joanna tattoos.

I wanted to give this tribute so that Joanna would know that she taught me how to read; that she's given characters, including herself, that will live within me forever; that I can never repay her for giving me the enduring academic chill.

I wanted to say, as Manley Pointer said to Mrs. Hopewell, "I hope you are well!"

I wanted to share this tribute so that the tide of darkness would sweep me back to her, postponing from moment to moment my entry into a world of guilt and sorrow.

I wanted this time to be with her. I wanted my chance for grace. I wanted to say that this good woman isn't hard to find—she's right here, with me, always.

But most all, I wanted to say, "Thanks."

Paul Gray

Never pompous or pedantic, he spoke with a twinkle behind everything he said. He always implied that it was fun to be talking, fun to be addressing the audience, fun to be playing with language. He knew how to make words bend to his liking, how to roll them from his tongue so that they might hang in the air for the taking, and how to sit on them when they wouldn't behave. He could force syllables into submission. He could corral consonants and order vowels. He could line up letters like bullets ready to be shot. Language, his loyal servant, listened when he spoke. His discipline was the weight of words. His style was applause for living.

I remember my anticipation, waiting for him to begin, for the pleasures of hearing his voice and the anger I would feel if time ran short and he would have to cut his remarks. But whenever he began, I was there, seduced. I would sit taking it all in, from the history he would reveal that would remind me of my naiveté to the poems he would explicate through his readings and his carefully constructed arguments that would show me how much I had missed. Whether he was discussing the old elocutionists and interpreters such as Thomas Sheridan, S. S. Curry, Gertrude Johnson, and especially Wayland Parrish or performer/poets such as Vachel Lindsay and James Whitcomb Riley, he brought to the task a respect, a willingness to assume that those he chose to examine would become most present when met with generosity. With people, he was always generous; with ideas, he could chew through stupidity like a dog might a bone. His way was an example for me to follow, to emulate. I work as an apprentice to a master.

And now, I brag: Once he asked me for a copy of a paper I had written. Perhaps his request was just a gesture of kindness or a desire to locate a reference I had cited, but I allow myself to believe that he wanted to read what I had written. That marvelous man wanted to read my words, and I could hope for no happier home for them than on his tongue.

Sherry Dailey

She will always be in that circle, that circle of school desks with the one she would occupy like a thin flower too tall for its vase; that circle of festival participants she had invited year after year to Indiana State University to celebrate the performance of literature, to explore themes she embraced and despised, and to gather around in the spirit of the generous question; that circle of friends who knew they were a part of something because they were connected to her, who would always circle back to her, who wanted to be in her presence; that circle that watched her prove Kenneth Burke's claim that literature is "equipment for living" by quoting lines from such poets as Howard Nemerov or e. e. cummings to make us all understand what we had been missing; that circle, honoring what the undergraduate student might say as well as what the guest speaker might share, learned how to behave by her model; that circle that always had room for one more chair, one more idea, one more act of kindness; that circle cannot be circumscribed, but it included me and changed forever my faith in *pi*; that circle's beginning and ending is in her.

She will always be across the dinner table, perhaps in that Italian restaurant, sipping wine, surprising the waiters with her Italian, and, between the antipasto and the ricotta-stuffed cannoli, moving from topic to topic as if she were checking off items on a grocery list, where we could have chatted for hours if only there were enough time. With the elegance of a ballerina straightening her sleeve, she would decide when everything was in its proper place, when all that need be said was said, when it was time to go. And I would leave, stunned by the brilliance of it all.

Carolyn Ellis

Helplessly attached to being human,[2] Carolyn Ellis, a poet of the everyday, seems unable to remove herself from her body. She seems incapable of accepting the arithmetic of it all. She thinks that the analysis of an individual's variance will not tell anyone anything meaningful about that individual, that a null hypothesis predicting sameness forgets those who do not curve under the bell, that the square root of abstract pronouncements is nothing more than more of the same. She is, I must report, trapped in her body. That's how she sees, with those intense eyes focusing on you, holding you in your place, making you want to say more. That's how she listens, accepting you, letting your joys and pains slide into her. That's how she feels, reaching out, always out, before she brings you into her open heart. Once there, you are hers, caught in sinews of her being. She cannot let you go. She cannot let herself be otherwise.

Helplessly attached to being human, she is wise to the other, the other who stands back, content, watching from a distance and the other who lives in the debris of daily living and dying. Her wisdom shows when she resists the critical eye for the open heart, when she rejects the antiseptic for the messiness of human lives, and when she turns from the decimal point of calculus to the decimal point of the tear duct. Her wisdom shows when she writes of her first husband and their final negotiations, of her brother's sudden death in an airplane crash, and of a friend who died of AIDS. In her sociology of dying, we come to understand life. Her wisdom shows when she calls us to "emotional sociology," to "evocative autoethnography," to "personal narratives," for she knows that in such tellings, we might find ourselves, might find what matters, and might find each other.

Helplessly attached to being human, she is there, looking, seeing what is there to see. She is there, feeling, experiencing what is there to experience. She is there, being, doing what is there to do. She comes to the page as a good priest comes to confession, leaning toward the window we might open. She is ready to listen. As she says in her own words:

> I begin to read, looking forward to being engaged. I let the words and images flow through me, eagerly anticipating what path the narrative will carve. Optimally, I want to think and feel with the story. . . . I want to be immersed in the flow of the story, lost in time and space, not wanting to come to the end (as in a good novel), and afterwards unable to stop thinking about or feeling what I've experienced. (273)

She comes to the page as empathy's emissary. This envoy of the heart moves between sensibilities, giving us messages of how to be. She comes to the page as a doctor feeling for a pulse, dissecting only to make whole again. She comes as encouragement's teacher.

Helplessly attached to being human, she teaches us what it means to live life every day, what it means to live with one's eyes wide open, what it means to be present. And with each encounter she and I have had, she has been present to me. The first time was over lunch during the period of all that talk about "Sextext." We spoke together sharing thoughts and impressions, but the point is this: She made me feel that the few little things I had to offer were worth hearing, that she cared about what I had to say, that I mattered. The last time we spoke was over a problematic book manuscript I had written. Then too, as has been my experience with every interaction we've had, she made me feel that the few little things I had to offer were worth hearing, that she cared about what I had to say, that I mattered.

Helplessly attached to being human, she is coming forward, trying to connect with us. Look, she is almost here. Be ready. She is in her body. Smile. She comes as a lesson for us all. She comes as a gift. Let's unwrap her now, together.

How to Become One of Us

Keep driving in, day after day, early when necessary. Find a parking place. Go up to your too-small office and open the door.

Notice that you can't fit another file folder in any of your four-drawer or five-drawer file cabinets. Promise yourself at the end of every semester that you will clean out the materials you no longer need. Pretend there are some materials in there that you do need.

Lunch with your colleagues. See how much better the food tastes when you are chewing on ideas rather than other colleagues.

Say casually over lunch that PowerPoint is nothing more than the latest version of an overhead projector and that, as far as you are concerned, overhead projectors were never quite as effective as a good piece of chalk and a clean blackboard.

Live for the pleasures of the classroom. Feed on its promise, its energy, its demands. Enjoy the work of being there.

Understand why you can't make yourself throw or give away that 1961 4th edition textbook for the basic course. Cherish all the books on your shelf that you planned to read but never did. Live in fear that you are stacking books precariously high on top of your three bookshelves.

Resist using old lectures, no matter how well they first worked. They will never work as well again, will never have again the driving passion of their creation, will never be again anything more than leathery dried fruit.

Regret that there is no disability insurance for paper cuts.

Watch your vitae grow, even without padding. Ask yourself if you would get tenure if you applied to yourself the same criteria you use to judge others. Ask yourself whether you would merit tenure if one selected any six consecutive years on your vitae. Ask yourself if your colleagues, if given a second chance, would vote for you again.

Have a designated space in your office where you place things you are supposed to and intend to handle but that you will be able to throw away without any consequences if you wait long enough.

Accept that you cannot read without holding a pencil in your hand. Develop your own system for marking the important points you want to remember. Think of your system as aesthetic.

Know that you can toss, without reading, the minutes from any university meeting. Avoid participation on the Faculty Senate and Graduate Council unless, of course, you like to doodle on yellow tablets while speaker after speaker says things with great intensity that don't matter and unless, of course, your program is the subject of conversation.

Believe that the scholars who review your work wish you no harm. Wish no harm to the scholars whose work you review.

Long for the time in your life when e-mail did not consume at least an hour of your life every day. Try not to laugh when people say that e-mail saves time and when people claim that the 'Net is a terrific vehicle for research.

Flip through your grade books, all of them, and see how few of your students you remember, even the ones who made A's and the ones who made F's, even the ones who were border cases and who kept you awake as you struggled to decide what to do. Be embarrassed.

Take comfort in the fact that no matter what drawer in your desk you might open, you can find a paper clip.

Lament over how the scholars with whom you cut your critical teeth are now dismissed with a simple turn of a phrase, as if everyone now knows that they have and have had nothing to offer, as if everyone has read them, as if everyone believes that you were silly to have wasted your time with such naïve ideas.

Recognize that distance learning is as good an idea as televised learning was.

Study who is hot and be impressed. Resist thinking that what is being argued is just another version of what was argued thirty years ago. Recognize that the reading list you had to master in graduate school has none of the same sources current graduate students must master.

Fear the commodification of higher education. Cringe when colleagues make arguments based on FTEs just as quickly as deans, when economic gurus without academic credentials are hired as university presidents, when students only want to know how much money they might make if they major in your field. Cringe when higher education is run like Wal-Mart, as if we are all shopping for the best prices in town.

Continue to worry, as you have for thirty years, about the number of jobs in the field. Count the positions lost; count the positions gained. Read the job listings in *Spectra* by searching for the right words.

Acknowledge that the union is responsible for getting some extra money into your pocket. Consider the cost.

Write in the hope that you are at least half as interesting as those you quote. Select those you quote carefully, preferably from those you have read. Quote yourself only to point out the error of your earlier thinking. Be grateful when, correctly or not, you are quoted.

Read. Read some more. Know that you can never catch up. Wear your stu-pidity like an old pair of shoes that still hurt your feet.

Learn before it's too late in your career the two keys to happiness within the academy: (1) No matter how seemingly justified, never say anything against a colleague and (2) No matter how seemingly justified, never say anything against a colleague's area, for to do so is to say something against a colleague.

Count the years you've been teaching and realize that you have been at it more years than there are years to your retirement. Think of retirement as a time when there are no papers to grade, when there are no committee meet-ings to attend, when there are no departmental review reports to write. Think of retirement as a time when you have no students and you have no reason to drive in.

Notes

1. Joanna Maclay is a noted scholar and performer of the works of Flannery O'Connor. Each paragraph in this tribute references an O'Connor story as it praises the life of this wonderful teacher.

2. I borrow this phrase from William Stafford, who uses it in a tribute to the poetry of Raymond Carver.

Works Cited

Ellis, Carolyn. "Creating Criteria: An Ethnographic Short Story." *Qualitative Inquiry* 6 (2000): 273–77.

Stafford, William. "Suddenly Everything Became Clear to Him: Remembering Raymond Carver." *Crossing Unmarked Snow: Further Views on the Writer's Vocation.* Eds. Paul Merchant and Vincent Wixon. Ann Arbor: University of Michigan Press, 1998.

CHAPTER 15

The Academic Tourist:
A Critical Autoethnography

Students just keep coming and you think you will remember them, but most of them fade, like the class lectures you keep using, even though you always plan on writing new ones with new ideas and new strategies that will make for an even better class (and sometimes you do), but mostly you rework what you've done, copying again what you know has worked and hoping you can bring enough enthusiasm to teach this once again, and you figure since there is nothing but new faces out there, it really doesn't matter, but you really think it does, but you just don't have the time to do anything about it, so there you are standing in front of the class saying what you've said before, caring about what you are saying but feeling a little bored and trying not to show it and having said it so many times that you have forgotten how it might be complex, because it surely isn't for you anymore—it's more like the Lord's Prayer or the Pledge of Allegiance, which you can recite without thinking—but you sense that they aren't getting it or that they don't want to get it, so you try explaining it in a new way and you find yourself getting excited about the ideas, and in the middle of what you take to be the key point, a student asks if this will be on the test, and you feel tired, but you push on, thinking about how the test in your file drawer can be adapted to make sure this will be on the test, and you're glad that you only have fifteen more minutes before the bell will ring, and when it does, you rush to say a few last things, as if it mattered, and then you leave, chalk dust on your pants and fingers, knowing that you've only scratched the surface of the subject and knowing too that at a time when education is more about packaging, more about FTEs, more about supplying the economy with a labor force to build the American industrial complex, little is likely to be complex; instead, your lectures are postcards from the classroom, your supportive words are photographs to be placed in the family album, and the diplomas you hand out at the end of the year are souvenirs for hanging on the wall and you are, at best, the tour guide who really never knew your way around, and as you begin again, you will see again what everyone else sees, you will go down the same path that everyone else takes, and you will know that you could read more—it's surely available—but you probably won't, because who wants to read an article when *Friends* is on or when friends are available for a drink or when you could just be taking a nap, so you will use that old script you learned long ago, the one that has you saying things that everyone takes for granted and keeps most students from asking any questions, but even if they do, you have a ready answer that you learned long ago—until the semester comes to an end and you let yourself believe that much has been accomplished which, of course, gives you permission to do it all over again because the students just keep coming.

And when you are not teaching, you're asked to do service for your department, university, community, or professional organizations, which often simply means that you're asked to sit in committee meetings and, like everyone else, to take your work too seriously, since most of the decisions the committees are supposed to address have already been made, but you go and listen and try not to play with your pen to a point of distraction since you do want to be a good citizen, really, but it's hard when you have so little information and no funds and no power to make anything happen and you do want to do your share because it just wouldn't seem right to say no, and there are some things that you do think matter, like who should get a university fellowship or who should be tenured or who should become chair of your department—such things impact your daily life so you're glad when you have some voice—but often when you're sitting there you think that you just don't have good criteria for making a good decision, partly because you don't have enough information and there is nowhere to get it and partly because any single decision seems to get swallowed in the complexity of the university system, so you try to fulfill your service obligations by doing things in the community and you discover that the university really doesn't want you to do that; it only wants enough done so that it might appear to have a great working relationship with the community, and in that desire, it creates programs, such as Service

Learning, that seem to establish a great working relationship with the community, but actually they just exploit students, which you aren't necessarily against if it is for a good cause, because you want to think that your work matters in the world, that you can be of some service to someone, even though you're not sure how what you have to offer is useful in the greater scheme of things, but you push on, knowing the arguments you've used to justify what you do and hoping that your arguments carry more truth than your feelings, and you accept that you'll probably never be able resolve your uneasiness, and you accept that service doesn't really count anyway, and you accept that you really rather not be doing it, particularly when *Friends* is on or when you could be having a drink with your friends or when you could just be taking a nap.

And when you are not doing service for your department, university, community, or professional organizations, you are supposed to be doing research, such as writing a paper like this one, since you are supposed to be a scholar and scholars do research; research that is supposed to develop a particular argument like the one in this paper that asserts that academics function as ethnographic tourists in that they, like tourists, like ethnographers, never get beyond the surface of things, even when they spend a lifetime at their sites, partly because lifetime habits of participant-observation are perhaps more blinding than initial participant-observation, partly because the work academics should do is just too hard to do given that most only live into their seventies or eighties, and partly because academics, in their greatest display of arrogance, think that they can get beyond the surface of things, and scholars do research that is supposed to look a certain way and you know that this paper isn't one of the ways because you don't have any quotes and a friend of yours just recently said, without meaning to be critical, that she wished she could do your kind of research because then she wouldn't have to go to the library, but you heard it as critical and so you begin to think of who you might quote and you remember one of your favorite lines in "A Hippocratic Oath for the Pluralist" from Wayne C. Booth's book *Critical Understanding: The Powers and Limits of Pluralism* that reads, "I will publish nothing, favorable or unfavorable, about books or articles I have not read through at least once" (351), but you feel a little guilty using it since you've use it before and it is a fairly dated source—1979—but you believe it is still relevant since you know you are guilty of breaking the oath, an oath you believe in, but you wonder what does it mean to have "read" someone, such as Derrida for instance, who you've quoted but only read in translation, only read all of a few of his many books and parts of a few others, read some summary books on his books, and read without fully understanding everything you encountered, so you wouldn't want to claim that you have more than a partial grasp of his work, if that; even still, you know the tradition of quoting that is supposed to prove you know something and you know that you aren't doing enough of it here to prove your case so you think you might cite some of the giants in ethnography, such as Gerry Philipsen, Dwight Conquergood, or James Clifford, but then you remember what Clifford wrote in *Routes: Travel and Translation in the Late Twentieth Century*:

> A certain degree of autobiography is now widely accepted as relevant to self-critical projects of cultural analysis. But how much? Where is the line to be drawn? . . . Writing an ethnography of one's subjective space as a kind of complex community, a site of shifting locations, could be defended as a valid contribution to anthropological work. It would not, I think, be widely recognized as fully or characteristically *anthropological* in the way that work in the externalized *field* still is. One could hardly count on being awarded a Ph.D., or finding a job in an anthropology department, for autobiographical research. (88)

and you know you sure don't want to quote him, even though you don't think you're writing autobiography; maybe you're writing autoethnography, which lets you use yourself to get to culture, but these distinctions get blurry, and so you decide to just forget the whole quoting thing, even through you know you could cite scholars such as H. L. Goodall, Jr., Carolyn Ellis, or Norman K. Denzin that would support what you are trying to do, and as you are making that decision, you flash on another way to write this paper that turns the speaker of the essay explicitly into a tour guide:

> Step right up, ladies and gentlemen. Step right up. See the academic in the front of the room reading his paper, his eyes buried on the page and his nervous hands shaking, mumbling on and on in words and sentences that never seem to end. He is typical of his kind. Notice too those who are also in the room. A few nod now and then, trying to show some interest, but most are restless in their straightback chairs. They are anxious for everything to be over so they can get some lunch or visit with an old friend. Later, over dinner, they will have forgotten what they heard, so they will spend their time gossiping about others of their kind.

and you think that the tour guide strategy might work, but you have already written more than you planned to write, and you know you are pushing the amount of time you have for presenting an essay in this or that style, and you really don't want to start over, and then Barbara Kirshenblatt-Gimblett's claim that display constitutes its subject comes rushing toward you, and you wonder if you have become what you have argued and you know that if you let yourself, you'll feel depressed, but you also believe with her that "[t]he first order of business is . . . to examine critically the conventions guiding ethnographic display, to explicate how displays constitute subjects and with what implications for those who see and those who are seen" (78), and you think you are doing that, at least implicitly; but you don't want to get into it any farther than you have, at least not now, because *Friends* is on and you plan on having a few drinks with your friends a bit later and you are hoping to get in a nap before then.

And just when you decide you're finished, just when you're feeling pleased with yourself because you managed to come back for the magical third time to that line about *Friends*, and you feel you've made your case about how academics, like tourists, never see the world beyond its surface level, your friend, the one who made that comment about citations, comes by and you tell her your argument, and she says, as if she were quoting a line straight from T. S. Eliot's "The Love Song of J. Alfred Prufrock," "That is not it at all" and goes on to suggest that the concept of tourist takes its definition in the notion of leaving home and your argument centers on seeing in a superficial way while at home and you believe she is right and her remark gets you wondering what reviewers might say if you ever decide to send this paper out, and you imagine them wanting you to consider the tourism research that tries to take away the easy dismissal of tourism as necessarily problematic even though that misses the point of your paper, and you feel exhausted but you want more than anything else for this essay to be off your desk and you think that you'll just cancel having a drink with your friends tonight and that you'll just take a nap because you're feeling tired, even though *Friends* is on.

Works Cited

Booth, Wayne C. *Critical Understanding. The Powers and Limits of Pluralism.* Chicago: University of Chicago Press, 1979.

Clifford, James. *Routes: Travel and Translation in the Late Twentieth Century.* Cambridge: Harvard University Press, 1997.

Franklin, A. "Performing Live: An Interview with Barbara Kirshenblatt-Gimblett." *Tourist Studies* 1 (2001): 211–32.

Kirshenblatt-Gimblett, Barbara. *Destination Culture: Tourism, Museums, and Heritage.* Berkeley: University of California Press, 1998.

CHAPTER 16

Schooling in Classroom Politics

Frank's[1] argument was deeply felt and simple: Jesse Ventura, governor of Minnesota, proved he did not believe in freedom when he claimed in an interview in *Playboy Magazine* that religion is a crutch for the weak-minded. Frank's argument unfolded in the following syllogism:

Good Christian people came to this country for their freedom.

By saying Christians are weak-minded, Ventura spoke against good Christian people.

Therefore, Ventura must be against freedom.

How could an elected governor believe such a thing, how could he speak in such a manner, how could we allow our morals to lapse to such an extent? Frank's outrage was evident; his core sense of proper moral behavior was threatened. I knew that I would not be able to convince him that the internal and external validity of his claims were suspect. So I simply said: I am outraged as well. My ethical code tells me that one should not insult so many weak-minded people.

No, I didn't say that, but I admit it was my desire. I wanted to strike at the stupidity, to expose it for what it was. I wanted to separate myself as far away from the logic of this utterance as I could. I wanted to mark him as my enemy. My job, however, was to help him. My job was to aid the enemy.

Teaching is political.

When it was her turn to perform, Amanda Grove came on stage and read the National Endowment for the Arts mission statement:

> The mission of the National Endowment for the Arts is to foster the excellence, diversity, and vitality of the arts in the United States and to help broaden the availability and appreciation of such excellence, diversity, and vitality. In implementing its mission the Endowment must exercise care to preserve and improve the environment in which the arts have flourished. It must not, under any circumstances, impose a single aesthetic standard or attempt to direct artistic content.

She then led us, without explanation, outside the building. Dressed in black and blindfolded was a large man holding a whip. Beside him was a pan of black paint, and nearby the NEA mission statement was printed on canvas, perhaps 7' by 10'. The audience gathered in a circle and Amanda moved from audience member to audience member asking, "What do you find obscene?" When someone answered, she'd ask for a dollar from that person, dip the dollar in her own red paint, and write with the dollar what the person said on the canvas while the blindfolded man in black, his whip soaked in black paint, struck out randomly and fiercely at the canvas. Amanda, barely dodging the blows of the whip, continued to write. With each crack of the whip, the audience would wince, fearing Amanda would be hit, and with each crack of the whip, the audience would back away, protecting itself from the flying paint. No one intervened.

When it was time for the class to discuss the performance, I was profuse. I went on and on about how exciting I thought this performance was, how it put into play such compelling issues, including the relationship between money and the arts, from how money becomes a form of censorship to how willing we were to pay just a dollar to have our own views about obscenity expressed, including the risks, symbolized by the violent whip, that artists take in a culture that has such little value for the artists, risks not only for themselves but on behalf of all of us, including our own culpability, our own indifference, our own actions that put us in safe places, and our own smugness. I used the performance as an opportunity to say that according to *High Performance* in 1996, the per capita cost of the NEA to U.S. taxpayers in 1995 was 38 cents, that the percent of the federal budget taken by the NEA last year was less than 1/100th of 1 percent, and that the number of Americans in every 100 making their living through the arts is 1.4. If anything, I argued, the federal dollars spent today are less now than they were then. And still I went on, saying how this is the kind of performance I was hoping for in this class. I encouraged everyone to be more like Amanda and, without saying so explicitly, more like me.

Teaching is political.

I ask my class how many Republicans are in our midst. Several brave souls raise their hand. I didn't know, I tease, that there were that many unethical people in the room. How do you sleep at night, I asked, still teasing, knowing that your beliefs are harmful to so many people in the world? How do you look at yourself in the mirror? They know I'm joking and they know I'm not.

Teaching is political.

A student writes a short analysis paper of the Langston Hughes poem "Theme for English B" in preparation for his class performance. The essay is about half the length I had asked for, filled with numerous grammatical errors and structural problems and lacking in detailed argument, but it manages to capture a sense of the student's appreciation of the piece. He shows why the poem matters to him and that, I reason, should be rewarded. I grade the essay a B-. After getting the grade back, the student is upset and comes to my office to complain. I try to point out all the problems with his writing, problems I have carefully marked and described on his essay. I try to tell him what I think are the strengths of the essay, again repeating what I had written. I try reading the poem with him, showing aspects of the piece that he might have explored in greater depth, but about midway through, he pushes his chair back and says: "I know why I made a B-." I look up, anxious to hear his explanation. He points to his skin. In the hard silence that follows, my eyes fall on Hughes's lines:

Sometimes perhaps you don't want to be a part of me.
Nor do I often want to be a part of you.
But we are, that's true.

Teaching is political.

A friend of mine led me through an etymological analysis of the common phrase "that sucks." Convinced by his arguments that link the negative valence of the phrase with a gay sensibility, I decided I would eliminate using the phrase in my own talk. Shortly after making this promise to myself, a student in class used "that sucks" as a summary comment to several arguments in a speech. I felt I needed to suggest during the critique session why some members of his audience could find the phrase objectionable. I moved slowly, knowing that the audience might be resistant to this idea, might feel it is just another example of political correctness running rampant, might rally in defense of the speaker. My fears were well founded; they argued that the phrase is not in any way connected to gays, that it does not give offense, that they see no reason to stop using it. I stood there, feeling inadequate. I was unable to make a convincing argument. It was as if I had skipped several chapters they needed to know before they would be ready for this case. And I stood there, thinking that we teachers are the ones who managed to make students so skeptical of such ideas.

Teaching is political.

"These are the books for the class," I say. "You must select the literature you'll be performing from one of these two books."

"These are the assignments for the class," I say. "You must complete all assignments in order to pass the course."

"These are the guidelines for attendance for the class," I say. "If you don't come to class, you can lose up to 10 percent off your final grade."

"These are readings for the class," I say. "Participation is part of your attendance grade."

"These are my style preferences for your writing assignments for the class," I say. "Please follow them carefully."

"These are the kind of tests I give for the class," I say. "If you take good notes, you shouldn't have any problems."

"These are the grading criteria for the class," I say. "Notice what you would have to do in order to earn an A."

"These are the days I won't be able to meet with the class," I say. "During those class periods that I cannot be here, use your time productively."

"These are the course objectives," I say. "I'll expect each of you to meet these goals."

"Do you have any questions?"

Teaching is political.

I call them "the Caps," those young men who sit in the back wearing their favorite team's insignia, pulled down to just over their eyes. Cool and cautious, they seem afraid to show what they know and what they don't. I encourage them to participate in the classroom discussion, and they do what they feel they must, nothing more. Their bodies hang in their chairs, sure they will find nothing of interest here, sure only of the space they are guarding. They wait out the hour, listening for the bell to ring. They make me feel as insecure as they are.

Teaching is political.

Elizabeth Whitney's one-person show placed her femme lesbian persona on stage to discuss gay and lesbian politics. In the discussion that followed, some argued that Elizabeth's appealing personality made the politics easy for the audience to handle. "Cute" was the operative word. "You were so cute, how could anybody have trouble with what you were saying?" was the often-repeated response. Others, however, argued that even though Elizabeth was "cute," the show was still risky. Eighteen-year-old men, in particular, were held up as the most likely to be unsympathetic to the show's themes. "These ideas," some posited, "would make eighteen-year-old men quite hostile." I felt a need to rally to the defense of those poor eighteen-year-olds. "I don't think they would be hostile," I began. "It's just as likely that they would be turned on. They probably were thinking about how to find another femme as 'cute' as Elizabeth for a grand threesome."

Teaching is political.

"I don't know why we have to analyze everything so much," Jessica said, feeling that a performance she thought quite moving was being yanked away from her by the force of our critical commentary. I gave her the standard academic answer about importance of critical reflection, about the need for criticism for artistic development, about the ideological implications of just accepting what comes our way. I gave her everything I could, but I couldn't keep her from feeling robbed.

Teaching is political.

Jim loved every performance he ever saw. He would go on and on about the performance he had just seen, pointing to particular things that he found just amazing. After watching him in several classes, I became convinced that he was sincere. He truly thought performance was an occasion for celebration. One day, after he seemed even more exuberant than usual, I said that I would like to see him give just one performer just one suggestion for improvement by the end of the semester. My comment embarrassed him, but he said he would try. The next class he offered a little suggestion, surrounded by numerous qualifiers that it was just his opinion and that he could easily be wrong.

Everyone in class could see how painful it was for Jim to submit even the most gentle of suggestions. Watching Jim struggle with my request, we found ourselves laughing. We could not help it. Jim was embarrassed again. In retrospect, I know now what I didn't understand then: My request embarrasses me.

Teaching is political.

Jenny was a bright, wholesome, all-American student whom I thought had considerable potential. She had a keen analytic mind that could cut through to the allure and insidiousness of popular culture. I stopped her after class one day and asked if she were considering graduate school. "No," she replied, "I'm getting married and going to live in Kuwait. It will be such an adventure." "Yes, it will," I say hiding the fact that I doubt if the adventure will be a happy one. "Best wishes."

Teaching is political.

Latalya says she wants to make a difference. She says the reason she is in school is so that she can learn how to use performance to make the life of African Americans better. She says she is committed to her work. I say that the voices that I think make the most difference are those that encourage dialogue between the races. Latalya says that is not her interest.

Teaching is political.

Lynn came into my office and asked, "Do you mind if I close the door?" I did, but I felt I had no choice but to say that it was fine. She wanted, I was sure, to complain about a teacher, a friend of mine, for the fourth time. Her complaint was always the same. Lynn believed that he was sexually harassing her. He was, according to Lynn, looking at her in class longer than he did other students. "He was," Lynn said, "eyeing me."
"Has he ever approached you after class or said anything inappropriate to you?" I inquired the first time she made the charge. Knowing my friend, the accusation was hard to believe.
"No, but I know he wants to."
"What makes you think that?" I asked, falling right into her logic.
"Because of how he looks at me in class."
Our first discussion lasted one hour. I outlined what formal courses of action she could take if she felt she was being sexually harassed. I talked about the possibility of dropping the class. I tried to show her support even though her story sounded suspicious to me. But each time I doubted her word I won-

dered if I were just perpetuating the patriarchal system that takes women's complaints of sexual harassment and turns those complaints into weapons against them. At the second conference, we repeated much of what was said the first time. I assumed she wanted to double check her options before deciding what to do, but as she talked I became increasingly skeptical about her charge. Convinced that Lynn's story could not be true, I said to my colleague over lunch in a tone that signaled my disbelief, "Your student Lynn thinks you're 'eyeing' her in class." "Well, she is an eyeful." The server appeared just then, and our conversation moved on to other things. We never spoke about Lynn again. The third time, her story, despite what my colleague had said, seemed even more implausible. She offered details that I just couldn't imagine my friend doing.

Now, here she was again, shutting the door and I wanted, more than anything else, for the door to remain open.

Teaching is political.

Ken speaks with passion about the inadequacy of the theory of evolution and the need to teach creationism in our educational system. To my mind, he presents fallacy after fallacy. Not a single argument seems sound. When it is time to critique his speech, I lead the class in a discussion of what a speaker would have to present to make this case persuasive. I note that speeches that take positions against majority views are particularly difficult. I try to be sensitive. Ken never returns to class again.

Taylor is the kind of student that I always find myself gravitating toward. He leads with his politics, often noting the social injustices in the world. He is quick to question, quick to debate. More often than not, I can hear myself arguing for the same things he does in his speeches. I often find myself chatting with him before class starts. I always enjoy those interactions. He never misses class.

Teaching is political.

When students come to class late without any prior explanation, I am usually aggravated. Their tardiness often is a disruption. I find myself stopping to catch the latecomers up on what's going on or ignoring the intrusion but feeling a bit guilty since I know they are probably confused about the ongoing discussion. If a student has a history of repeated tardiness, I'll penalize the student's participation grade. You can't participate, I reason, if you're not there, and by coming late, you disrupt others' participation. Other people's time, I was taught to believe, should be respected and, like all commodities worth having, should not be wasted. Time, after all, is money. But if you don't think of time as your own and if you have a history of others using your time to make their money, then you might come to class late as well.

Teaching is political.

I was already two class periods behind on the syllabus when the discussion broke out. The test was next week and I needed to cover three more chapters. I wanted to let them talk about what interested them. I was glad so many students were involved, some of whom seldom spoke. It was one of those wonderful exchanges when everyone is jumping in, when everyone believes something is at stake, when everyone is present. I saw all that and still I said, "We have to move on."

Teaching is political.

I've never met a teacher who didn't have stories that pointed to misused words in essays, silly comments made in class, questionable performance choices, and other student efforts ripe for mocking. I've even known teachers who keep a file of such mishaps. These tales from the field rely upon our arrogance for their comedy.

Teaching is political.

Once two people believe racism is at work, everything that is done and said is read through that lens. Once we make that assessment about each other, we can no longer teach each other.

Teaching is political.

I sometimes preface a comment in class with the line, "This is what I want you to know." Usually about half the class decides to write down what follows. Sometimes I'll say, "This is what I want you to know for the test." Then about 90 percent of the class takes notes. I can't remember a time when a student marked a question with, "This is what I want to know."

Teaching is political.

When I teach performance art, I encourage students to take risks, to question the conventional, to put their bodies on the line. And they have. They've stripped before their classmates to call into question the gaze; they've done physical harm to themselves and threatened their audiences to show what might be at stake; they've named names, confessed, and shared secrets to display our common humanity. And I have applauded, loudly, with each new stab at the familiar, the taken-for-granted, the status quo. I have applauded as they have taken what is possible in the class beyond my expectations. I have applauded as they created public selves that would never be seen in the same way again.

Teaching is political.

The personal is political, including the insistence that it be shared.

Teaching is political.

Stephanie Howell's performance was a powerful critical commentary about the ridicule and suffering that women face who exceed the ideal weight of contemporary standards. The performance culminated in a video clip where unspecified parts of Stephanie's body were written upon with derogatory words. Following the performance, I opened the class for discussion. Everyone was effusive, noting the power of the piece, its careful execution, its rhetorical force. Then Melanie, whose athletic body seems to match the ideal weight of contemporary standards, spoke. "This was a wonderful performance," she said. "It's important for all women to listen to what you had to say. I know because I was heavy. The story you told is my story too." She began to cry and could not go on. Stephanie went to her and held her. It was a perfect pedagogical lesson, a perfect response, a perfect human moment. I stood there, watching.

Teaching is political.

Jason Hedrick's bright eyes and quick smile coupled with his large body are part of his charm. He sees himself as a performer and as a writer; so does everyone else who knows him, perhaps because he has such an affinity for language. He understands how to work a line until it carries his deep voice. He can play with words until they make a thick, rich soup. Everyone expects more from him when he takes the stage than is fair to expect. So when he wheeled the video center stage, turned it on, and then left, we all assumed that something worth viewing would happen. What we saw was a video of an African American evangelist speaking in a heavy cadence with punctuated, audible breaths, a performance that seemed like a parody of the stereotypical Black preacher. The scene, it appeared, was a religious convention, held in a large, mostly empty, auditorium. The few who were in attendance seemed to be ignoring his remarks, some just walking by and others just chatting among themselves.

As I watched the tape play on that dark stage, I, being the white liberal that I am, became increasingly uncomfortable with what Jason, a white student, was doing. I uttered a quiet, disapproving groan. I whispered to my colleague sitting beside me that this didn't seem right. I squirmed in my seat. The tape went on and on. I felt angry, embarrassed, impatient. I did not go on stage to turn the tape off, although in retrospect I wish I had. After about twenty minutes, the curtain closed and the preacher's voice finally faded.

I wanted to tell Jason how problematic I thought it was to place that video of that Black evangelist on stage before a predominately white audience. I wanted to argue that pulling the evangelist out of his cultural context was culturally insensitive, disrespectful. I wanted to say that even if the intent was to make the audience reflect about their own prejudices and stereotypes, that goal was at the expense of the evangelist, who was turned into a freak and put on display for our amusement. I wanted to say what was done was wrong, but I said nothing. Perhaps I was silent because I assumed that Jason had something in mind that I was missing that would redeem the performance or because I didn't want to do the hard work of that conversation or because I felt I didn't have the right to offer such a harsh critique since Jason wasn't my student that semester or because the opportunity to discuss the performance never presented itself or because my white liberal knee was jerking so predictably, so safely, so smugly that I was afraid to begin the dialogue.

Teaching is political.

Karen's poems spoke of her dedicated love, a love so strong that she would "rather die" without it, a love so pure that she is sure it was "made in heaven," a love so true that she'll never "be blue." After reading them, I suggested that she might want to be more concrete, to offer the reader specific images, to find fresh metaphors. "But that would ruin it," she said. I nodded, thinking that sometimes reflection does indeed ruin it.

Teaching is political.

When their papers come in I grade them, usually not in red but with the kinder gray of pencil. I try to be helpful. I point out grammatical errors, poor organizational structures, and faulty reasoning. I know what A papers look like. I know what we privilege. I know who will be least likely to write one.

Teaching is political.

A review sheet had been given. The test consisted of 25 multiple-choice, 10 definition-of-terms, and 5 short-answer questions. The answers came from class lectures and the six assigned chapters from the textbook. Grades fell into a perfect distribution: three A's, five B's, six C's, two D's, and two F's. There were right answers.

Teaching is political.

Is there a time when you must say to a student that you believe he/she will not succeed in college? Is there a time when you say that not because the student has acted irresponsibly but because you just don't think the student is smart enough to do the work? Is there a time when you wonder if that is your failure?

Teaching is political.

You can't climb the ladder of success if you don't have a ladder; you can't pull yourself up by your bootstraps if you don't have any boots; you can't put your nose to the grindstone if you don't have a stone.

Teaching is political.

Zach, a Baptist preacher who was returning to school after many years to complete his undergraduate degree, decided to give his persuasive speech against a woman's right to an abortion. He was a skilled speaker and knew how to build a case. In short, he gave the best persuasive speech I've heard from the pro-life perspective. Liz saw the speech not as an example of a speech that met the requirements of the assignment particularly well but as a speech that needed challenging. When he finished and started to return to his seat, Liz began: "I had an abortion. Don't you tell me that what I did was wrong, that I'll regret it all my life. You don't know anything about my life!" His answer came back quickly, not from the calm, reasoned stance of his speech but with a force of unleashed anger: "I'm just telling you what God says. You can't go against the word of God." "Here's what I think of your God," she retorted, picking up her public speaking textbook, the one that advocates the free exchange of ideas for the greater democratic good, and threw it at him. I entered the fray: "Maybe it's time to stop this dialogue." A tense quiet settled into the room. Then I added, "Let me just say that this is what I meant when I argued that speech matters."

Teaching is political.

Note

1. Throughout the essay, the use of only first names indicates a pseudonym; full names are real names.

CHAPTER 17

What the Heart Learns

O n a recent family trip to Gulf Shores, I asked my parents, "After living for eighty-five years, what would you say your heart has learned?" Speaking with the authority of those years, they both answered quickly. My mother, who spends her days playing with her computer despite the fact that her eyes require that the screen image be so large that only three or four letters at a time will fit, said, "To pump." My father, who has become increasingly forgetful, remembered what mattered to him most. He responded, "To love." After answering, they turned to me: "How would you answer your own question?" "I don't know," I replied, "but I like what you said. I guess if I had to give another answer, I'd say 'to forgive.'" Perhaps in those simple and sentimental claims the heart finds its method.

"To pump" suggests that we keep going, day after day, regardless of what we face. To keep pumping is an insistence on life, a refusal to give in, to succumb. It is a persistent desire to make sense of it all, to tell some story that will allow us a moment's rest. It is a claim to our right to take some small measure of space, to locate ourselves in relationship to others who are and are not like us. It is to say, "I exist." Knowing that the heart is still at work is our evidence.

"To love" tells how the pump works best. We have all read in magazine after magazine the medical claims: People in loving relationships are more likely to be healthy, more likely to describe their lives as happy and satisfying, more likely to be viewed positively by others. But it is just evidence that supports

WHAT THE HEART LEARNS | 163

what the heart learns. It learns by feel. When love comes, it beats in assuring rhythms, strong and full, letting us know we are alive. When love goes, it tightens, and pain, real as a knife's cut, slices across us. Little wonder that the heart might harden, that it might be held back by the cynic, that it might be the place where some say fools rush in. Yet is there another place to go? Can we find anyplace else that gives what the heart gives when it drums in concert with another? Are we brave enough to live without at least the hope of connection? Perhaps I am a fool to believe in such drivel. Perhaps if I didn't believe I'd be a larger fool.

"To forgive" tells what we must do if we are to love. No one is likely to always do what we might hope. Some do little of what we might wish. When others disappoint us, they seldom see themselves as the villains of their own stories. They have their reasons, their explanations. And even when they know they have done wrong and stand before us in hope of our generosity, they see their errors as a momentary lapse, as a flaw they wish they didn't have, as an act that should be forgiven. They see themselves as worthy of our compassion. To forgive is to recognize the messiness of being human and to position ourselves to be forgiven for our own human foibles. All of our mistakes have company. The more we learn to accept, the less there is to forgive.

The heart's method of pumping, loving, and forgiving encourages us to proceed with our hearts first. It asks that we remain engaged, encircling and embracing what is before us, as we struggle to understand and accept the enigma of human life. It is an act of empathic embodiment. This feeling into another through the body calls upon the cognitive to guide where the heart might go. It is not devoid of consideration. But it insists that what matters most to people is how a "what" might feel. How an idea can turn the stomach, a claim can shut the eyes, or a thought can make the head ache reminds us that the body knows how words feel when they speak. What matters is what the heart learns. And, perhaps not surprisingly, when we proceed with our hearts first, we discover that humans are at their best when they are pumping, loving, and forgiving.

Another Day at the Office: #1

When Dr. Elizabeth Martin came into my office and plopped down, I knew something was wrong. Liz is not a plopper. She moves through each day with efficiency, with purpose. She is always on to her next task but never lets her list of things to do, a list she makes first thing each day when she arrives at work, intrude on the time she is willing to give students.

"What's the matter, Liz?" I asked, looking up from an assessment report I was trying to finish.

"I just can't take it anymore," she answered. Her voice was weaker than I've ever heard it. Her tailored, dark-blue blazer hung slightly off her shoulder.

"What's the 'it'?" I said, not sure where we were headed. I knew she had just finished teaching a graduate class that had a student in it who wanted to challenge her every time he got a chance. I thought that might be the problem. "Did that ass in your methods class give you trouble again today?"

"Yes, but it's not just that. It's all of it—the stacks of papers that need grading, the theses and dissertations that must be read, the papers that have to get written, the students who act like asses and the students who don't but who want your time, the faculty meetings, the committees—all of it. It never ends."

"I know what you mean. It never does end," I said, gesturing to the stacks of papers on my messy desk.

"I want a life," she continued. "I don't want every waking hour consumed by this job." I sat there nodding. It was a complaint I'd heard many times by many other faculty. There is no doubt that doing the job right requires more than most want to give. Then she added, "I think I'm going to resign."

"You can't do that," I shot back, realizing for the first time what was at stake in this conversation. My mind raced through what it might mean if Liz did resign. Her advisees would be devastated. Her colleagues, too, would be devastated. They depend upon her, not only for the workload she carries and the quality of her talk but for the emotional health of the department. Scholars at other universities would see Liz's departure as a significant blow to the program. They send their best students to work with her.

"This isn't a sudden decision," Liz said. "I've been thinking about it for some time now."

"Please tell me you're not serious," I whined.

"Sorry. I am serious," she answered with more strength than I was hoping to hear. I should have expected that. If nothing else, Liz is a strong woman, a strength that I've loved from the first time I had her in class as a master's student, through the wonderful exchanges we had when she was my doctoral advisee, through her first job where her meteoric rise to the top of her field was nothing less than amazing. It was partly because of her strength that the department hired back one of our own graduates.

"Oh, Liz," I moaned. "What a loss that would be!"

"I don't think everyone would feel that way."

"I don't know of anyone who wouldn't," I added quickly.

"Do you know what our dear chair said to me during my annual review? 'It's good you published three pieces this year. Next year, shoot for four and place them in more mainstream disciplinary journals.' Can you believe that?"

"That is hard to believe," I answered, thinking of the old *I Love Lucy* show where Lucy and Ethel try to keep up with the chocolates coming down the conveyer belt at faster and faster speeds.

"It seems no matter what you do, it's never enough," she said.

"You know Lance wouldn't have said that if he didn't think you were capable of doing it," I said, wanting to defend Lance and support Liz at the same time. But I didn't help matters.

"That's what I mean," Liz asserted. "Lance is just part of the system, an exploitive system that demands more and more. It wants every drop of your blood, but I've given all I can give."

"I can't imagine this place if you're not here giving," I said. "You're right. You have given so much."

"Thanks. I appreciate that."

"I don't know of any other faculty member who is more loved by both students and faculty," I offered.

"Thanks," she said again and then added, "but even if that is true, I don't know if that is enough."

"That's no small thing," I said. "Do you realize how much you mean to everyone, me included, in this department? Do you realize how amazing you are?"

"But why are we doing this?" she asked. "Does any of our work really matter?"

"You know I think so," I answered. "I could bring in your students to do testimonials if you'd like. I could remind you of the impact of your research—your short article in the Patterson anthology is cited more than any piece I know; your piece on identity is always ranked as the best piece we read in my survey class; the book you're writing will change how people think about communication and class. I could go on and on. Your research has had a tremendous influence. And I could remind you of the weight your voice had in guiding the department into its current configuration."

"All that feels pretty empty right now," she said.

"You're probably just experiencing some burnout," I offered. "It's hard to keep doing what we do day in and day out. Maybe you just need to give yourself a day at the beach."

"I'm not happy," she responded. "A day at the beach won't fix that."

"Maybe not, but it couldn't hurt."

Then she blurted out: "I don't want to be you, caught up in some sick Protestant work ethic."

I was stunned. Her words felt like a slap. After a moment, I said, "You're not me. You're much better. Some faculty have the intelligence but lack ambition. Some have the ambition but lack intelligence. Some have the intelligence and the ambition but lack modesty and grace. But you have it all."

"Right now, I feel like I'm lacking everything."

"You may feel that way, but the evidence doesn't support your case."

After Liz left my office, I couldn't get our conversation out of my mind. I realized what an investment I have in Liz. I had long understood how central she is to the quality of the department and how much I truly care about her, love her, want her to be happy. What I didn't realize, though, is that she is the dream I offer in my classes every day. She is what I want my students to become. But if she isn't happy, if the best success story I know is so miserable that she wants to resign, what am I doing? I need Liz to love her job so I can love mine.

The next day I saw Liz, list in hand, moving quickly past my office. I was still trying to finish the assessment report. She called back over her shoulder, "Too many things to do. Thanks for yesterday. We'll talk later."

"Great," I shouted after her.

Another Day at the Office: #2

"Hi. I'm home," I called, tossing my book bag to the floor.

"I'm upstairs," Margo called back. "I'm just finishing up." I knew that meant she was writing and that I shouldn't disturb her unless there was some emergency. I dropped down on the sofa and shut my eyes. It had been one of those days. Neither class I taught had gone particularly well, the College of Liberal Arts subcommittee on recruitment had been a waste of time, and with all the interruptions, I hadn't gotten anything done. I opened my eyes and glanced at the bag full of work that I needed to do that night. Then I heard Margo's footsteps coming down the stairs.

"Look what I've got in my hand," she said, sounding pleased. "It's the final chapter of my book!" She held out her pages as one would a newborn child.

I took her chapter and asked, "It's done?"

"Yes," she sighed, "it's done. Oh, I have a little cleaning up to do, but I should be able to send it off by the end of the week."

"Oh, honey, that's just great!"

"It's done," she repeated.

"You must have figured out what to do with section three," I said, thumbing through the pages. "I know it was driving you crazy."

"I was trying to make section two do too much," she explained. "Once I realized that, section three fell into place." She took the chapter from my hands. She never wanted me to read her writing until she thought it was in perfect shape.

"I look forward to reading it," I said.

"I'll give you a copy of the whole thing as soon as it's ready."

"I'd like that. I really want to read it," I responded. "Should we open some wine to celebrate?"

"Sure."

"Red or white?" I asked, going into the kitchen. "I think we have both."

"White."

"White it shall be," I said. I opened the wine and poured two glasses. I was truly pleased for Margo. But to be honest, after the day I had had, I wasn't ready for her happiness. Her joy, I'm embarrassed to say, made my day seem worse. I was forcing myself to act happy. And I felt small. I wanted the support and comfort of a loving partner after a hard day and I wanted to join my loving partner in her delight without hesitation or pettiness. As I brought in the wine, I vowed I wouldn't let my day intrude on Margo's excitement.

"Here you go." I held out a glass of wine to Margo.

"Thanks," she said.

"May your book sell a million copies," I toasted. Then I added, "We could use the money."

"I doubt we'll be retiring soon off of this book," said Margo, remembering how few authors make any money from academic press books.

"You never know," I said.

"Yeah, I think I know," Margo rejoined.

"Regardless, you should feel terrific about finishing your second book."

"I do."

"That's quite an accomplishment," I said, raising my wine in toast again.

"Thanks," she said. "Remember when I was ready to toss the whole thing in the trash? If you hadn't come into my office when you did, I probably would have."

"I'm glad I was able to make a timely entrance," I replied.

"You often do," Margo said. "Thank you for helping me get through this."

"I didn't do anything, except maybe keeping you from throwing it away," I joked.

"You did more than that," Margo responded, refusing to let my joke stand. Changing directions, she said, "I've got an idea. Let's cut up some apples and cheese for dinner. I'm too tired to cook and I don't want to go out. I'm exhausted from sitting at that computer all day. We can nibble on apples and cheese and sip our wine all night. Maybe watch a movie."

"That sounds great, but I have work I have to do," I replied.

"What can't wait until tomorrow?" she asked.

"All the stuff I didn't get done at the office today," I answered, letting my crankiness from the day show. "Sorry, I didn't mean to sound grumpy."

"What happened that turned you into Mr. Grumpy Pants?" she teased.

"Just the usual," I said, remembering I didn't want to put my day on Margo.

"Well, I know how to fix those grumpy pants." She rose and went straight for my book bag. "Someone has stolen your bag," she said. "You might be able to find it in the morning locked inside the trunk of my car." Carrying my bag out to the garage, she added, "Before then, there is little chance of its recovery."

Margo has always had a wonderful playfulness about her. I couldn't help but smile. And she was right—everything I thought I had to do could wait until tomorrow.

When she came back in, she said, "You stay there. I'll be right back with some apples and cheese and some more wine. Do you want some crackers too?"

"That would be great," I called into the kitchen. She returned with all she had promised on a tray. We sipped and nibbled and talked about what we wanted to plant in the garden. After a while, we turned on the television. Margo flipped through the channels until she found an old science fiction monster movie, and I knew that would be her pick.

"Oh, look," she said. "It's Godzilla."

I stretched out on the couch and put my head in Margo's lap. "Really great choice," I teased.

"Do you know why I like these movies?" she asked, as she ran her fingers through my hair.

"No, why?"

"Because they are so bad you don't have to take them seriously," she said. "I love it when you can see the zipper on the monster costumes."

"That explains it," I laughed.

"Whoever were the monsters that made you grumpy today," she said, "you just imagine unzipping their costumes."

With that thought in mind, I smiled up at Margo. She was still stroking my hair. After a while, as I was dozing off, I heard, "We cannot let Godzilla take the city."

Another Day at the Office: #3

Bill Sanders had successfully completed his preliminary examinations and was trying to take the next step toward finishing his degree. He came into my office with a list of faculty he wanted for his dissertation committee. He sat down and peeked inside a spiral notebook he was carrying. He wanted to check his list once again. He slowly looked up until his eyes met mine.

"I've decided on my dissertation committee," he said.

"That's good," I replied. "It's time for you to do that."

"I want you to continue as my chair?" he said, more as a question than a statement.

"I'd be glad to do that, Bill," I answered, "but you know you don't have to stay with the same chair after you complete prelims." Even though Bill would be another person to get through a dissertation, I really was happy to continue as his chair. We had a good working relationship. He was bright, careful, hard working, and, quite honestly, I would have been a little disappointed if he hadn't asked. But I wanted to make sure he didn't feel he was stuck with me.

"I know," Bill said. "It just makes sense to me if you continue, given where I'm going with my work."

These moments always feel a bit awkward to me. I don't want students to have to justify why they think I would be a good pick. So as soon as I'm sure a student knows that he or she has a choice and I know I'm willing to take the student on, I try to settle the question quickly.

"Okay. Great," I said. "Who else are you considering for your committee?"

Bill glanced at his notebook again. "Well, I want Dr. Martinez, Dr. Jones, and as my outside member, Dr. Golden from anthropology."

"Those are all great committee members. Good," I affirmed. "Who do you want for your third departmental member?"

"Dr. Dell."

"Dr. Dell?" I asked, making sure I had heard correctly.

"Yes," Bill answered and began a speech I'm sure he had rehearsed. "I've taken several classes with him and I think he would add a useful perspective. As I'm envisioning my dissertation now, his work would be really important to Chapter 3. I've heard," Bill continued carefully, "that you and Dr. Dell have had some difficulties in the past, but I'm hoping this could work out."

"Dr. Dell and I no longer serve on committees together," I responded flatly. "If you must have Dr. Dell, I'm afraid you'll have to find another chair. Have you considered Dr. Hogan? She brings many of the same things that Dr. Dell brings to the table."

"I guess she would be fine," Bill said, "but I really want Dr. Dell."

"Well, you think it over," I replied. "You don't have to make your decision today."

A week passed before Bill returned to my office. "I've been thinking about our discussion concerning my committee," Bill began, "and I don't see why I shouldn't be able to have the committee I want."

"I don't think the committee you want would be in your best interest," I said.

"But I don't see why you and Dr. Dell can't put aside your differences for the sake of your students," Bill pushed.

"It is for the sake of our students that we don't serve on committees together," I said, beginning to show some irritation. I felt that Bill was crossing a line.

"What if I talked with Dr. Dell to see how he would feel about being on the committee?"

"Bill," I said, "your job is to write a dissertation. Fixing relationships between faculty is not your job."

"This just doesn't seem right to me. Students shouldn't have to pick when both of you have so much to offer."

"Bill, from where you sit," I tried to explain, "there are things that you cannot understand. Faculty relationships often last longer than marriages and, given tenure, divorce is more difficult."

"What happened between you two?"

"It wouldn't be appropriate for me to share that, and even if I did, I'm sure Dr. Dell would have a quite different version." Wanting to put an end to this discussion that had gone farther than I thought it should, I added, "You just have to trust me when I say to you that it would not serve you well to have both of us on your committee."

"That's just wrong," Bill said, and he left.

The following week, the chair of the department, Dr. Grace Griffin, called me into her office. "I had a talk with Bill Sanders, who is upset that neither you nor Frank Dell are willing to serve on a committee together," she said, marking that she wanted me to be aware of Bill's complaint and, at the same time, indicating that she understood why Bill's demand could not be met.

"I did tell Bill that that combination wouldn't work," I said. "Did Frank say the same thing?"

"That's what Bill said."

"I can't believe that after the conversation I had with Bill he talked to Frank and then to you."

"He's insisting that he get the committee he wants," Grace said. "I told him that faculty have the right to decide if they want to be on a committee. I told him that it wasn't just his choice, but he kept going on and on about his rights. I'm pretty sure I told him many of the same things you did."

"I wonder why he doesn't get it."

"Bill's an idealist, not a realist," Grace replied.

"I guess you're right," I said.

"In some ways, he's right," Grace added. "It is a shame that you two have remained enemies all these years."

"I know," I said sadly. "One of my greatest surprises and disappointments in life is that I have accumulated several enemies. Frank is one of them."

"Perhaps it's hard not to collect enemies when you work in the academy," Grace said. "So many issues seem to get linked with self-worth and identity."

"Yeah," I sighed. "But I'm still not sure what I should do about Bill."

"I think the ball is in his court," Grace answered. "I just wanted you to know that he came to see me about this."

Several weeks passed and I hadn't heard anything from Bill. I didn't want Bill to stop his progress. I was worried about him. I thought about putting a note in his mailbox and asking him to drop by, but I wasn't sure if that was wise. Then one day he appeared at my door.

"Can I talk with you for a minute?"

"Sure Bill. Come on in."

"I'm fine here," Bill said. "I just wanted to tell you that I've formed my committee. Dr. Martinez has agreed to be my chair, and I've decided that it would be best if I didn't use you or Dr. Dell."

"I see."

"This hasn't been an easy decision for me," Bill added.

"Well, maybe that is the best solution," I replied.

"I think so," Bill said. "I'm sorry it didn't work out how I had originally hoped."

"I'm sorry too. Perhaps in a better world it would have. I do wish you the best of luck with your work."

"Thanks," Bill answered. He looked at me a moment longer. His brown eyes seemed darker, maybe sad. Then he turned and left.

Later that day in the copy room, I saw Frank Dell. "Hello, Frank," I said cautiously.

"Hello," he returned.

The Heart's Last Words

The heart learns that stories are the truths that won't keep still. There is always another version, another eye to tell what it sees, another voice ready to speak. They wiggle around until they become the deceptions we allow ourselves to keep.

My heart knows many tales, all true and all lies, all wanting to settle. But just when my heart thinks it has all the pieces together, everything falls apart. Like when my first wife and I went to see *The Way We Were* and before the movie started, she said she wanted a divorce because she was in love with my best friend. Like when my child who I haven't heard from in over a year calls for help from jail. Like when I discovered that a person who I thought was my friend was saying things about me that just aren't true. Like when I surprised myself by my own frustration at not having any answers.

The heart learns that facts are the possibilities we pretend we trust. We have little other choice. They are our best hunches, our best inklings. They allow for actions we believe will do no harm, perhaps even that might do some good.

I am a reader of signs. A glance, a quiet word, or a hand opening and closing may be all I have. I am always busy gathering, harvesting evidence. I want to trust. I want to swallow what I can name, what I can feel. So when I express my love for another, I do so with a cautious belief in the promise of connection. I accept the possibility that my heart knows its facts.

The heart learns that poems are the hypotheses that let our hearts pump, love, and forgive. We may struggle, unable to get the words of our poems right. We may fall short, incapable of finding our heart's rhythm. We may grind against ourselves, unskilled in locating healing comparisons. Poems, though, give our hearts permission and hope. They are open promises, waiting.

I am at a point in my career when people are beginning to ask if I'm planning to retire, but my heart's education continues. I know my heart still has much to learn. And so I go on, trying, one day at a time, to pump, to love, and to forgive; trying to walk, whenever necessary, on broken glass; to rejoice, whenever possible, in the stitch; to carry, whenever needed, the weight of the stone.

About the Author

RONALD J. PELIAS teaches performance studies in the Department of Speech Communication at Southern Illinois University, Carbondale. His previous books include *Performance Studies: The Interpretation of Aesthetic Texts*, *Writing Performance: Poeticizing the Researcher's Body*, and *The Green Window: Proceedings of the Giant City Conference on Performative Writing* (co-edited with Lynn C. Miller).